Praise for Stu Apte and *My Life in Fishing*

"Stu Apte has given us a rich collection of memories from the salmon waters of Ireland to the deck of Hemingway's boat. Witty, instructive, and engaging, this master of rod and reel is an angler's angler, and *My Life in Fishing* is the literary equivalent of a day in the flats on a school of permit."

—TOM BROKAW, former *NBC Nightly News* anchor and managing editor, host of *Buccaneers & Bones*

"I've made my living reading and editing the writings of others for decades, and most of the time the copy flowing past my desk looks much like any other. So imagine my surprise when Stu Apte sent me an advance copy of this gem, *My Life in Fishing*. Books like this don't often appear, with prose articulately relating insightful observations on our sport from a true innovator, combined with personal anecdotes and interactions with some of the most famous anglers of the twentieth century. *My Life in Fishing* represents more than a memoir; it's really an important history primer that belongs in the library of every serious angler. And by the way, it's a hell of a fun read, too."

—JOHN BROWNLEE, Editor-in-Chief, *Salt Water Sportsman* magazine

"Stu Apte remains an authentic legend: a man who has pursued his passion for catching big fish on light tackle the world over. His new book, *My Life in Fishing*, gives us a healthy dose of his legendary humor, while Stu shares some of his best stories of fishing from memorable fishing trips around the world with some of his famous friends. A great read!"

—DAVE BULTHUIS, Vice President of Sales, Costa Sunglasses

"With more than 60 years of fishing experience under his belt, Stu Apte has done and seen it all—from 200-pound-plus tarpon in the Florida Keys, to ten-pound brown trout in New Zealand, to salmon in Iceland and sailfish off Australia. Now he has gathered a lifetime's worth of angling tales in this one captivating book, *My Life in Fishing*, a book you're sure to enjoy, a book that will make you realize that, as Stu says, the good old days of fishing are right now. Don't let them get away!"

—JAY CASSELL, Editorial Director, Skyhorse Publishing

"Stu Apte's *My Life in Fishing* is an entertaining and educational collection of fishing stories told by one of the greatest anglers of our time, about his personal adventures and the legendary personalities he shared them with. It is a truly great read—I loved it!

Stu is also one of the Founding Directors of Bonefish & Tarpon Trust, and the Trust is grateful for all he has done and is doing for the future of our flats fisheries."

—TOM DAVIDSON SR., Chairman, Bonefish & Tarpon Trust

"I've known Stu Apte for more than 50 years. Through all these years, and in spite of his many other accomplishments, to me he is The Tarpon Tamer. He is responsible for cutting the time I used to fight big tarpon from a few hours to a few minutes. Thanks, Stu. But now Stu, who has taken just about every fresh and saltwater game fish on the planet, has a new book with many of his favorite stories and adventures. And I tell you, *My Life in Fishing* is a book you want to read. And reread. I know you are going to love it!"

—J.M. "CHICO" FERNANDEZ, fly fisherman

"I've known Stu Apte for a couple of decades now and have fished with him numerous times. I remember him setting a world record for fly rod tarpon in Key West back when the Navy had me stationed down there, circa 1971. But more vivid is the first time I actually saw Stu jump a tarpon on the fly, many years ago when we were fishing on Nine Mile Bank. There was nothing fancy about his casting—he just dropped the fly exactly where it was supposed to be. There was nothing fancy about his retrieve—it just made the tarpon want to eat a bunch of feathers. And watching Stu fight a tarpon—classic. His techniques are followed by all the best anglers, simply because they work. When someone asks me how I can land a 100-pound tarpon on a fly rod in 15 minutes, I tell them to get Stu's "Quest for Giant Tarpon" video and study it. No use trying to improve on perfection. Stu is the Willy Mays of fly fishing—

he makes everything look so easy, when everyone knows otherwise. *My Life in Fishing* will bring you right into the middle of Stu Apte's life in fishing, and there's really no better place to be."

—PAT FORD, photographer and author

"The rod-carrying, Pan Am 747 pilot has fished in every corner of the globe for six decades. Stu has caught every species there is to catch, and most of them on a fly rod. He has already achieved what every angler would love to do, but none started early enough in life to equal Stu's accomplishments. *My Life in Fishing* is a wonderful summary of some of Stu's amazing adventures, and reading the first few sentences makes you want to go fishing."

—GUY HARVEY, IGFA Hall of Fame, marine wildlife artist
   and conservationist

"Stu Apte is both a master angler and master storyteller. This marvelous book takes you to the world's greatest angling destinations, where epic encounters with all our favorite game fish unfold in perfectly calibrated color and detail. I felt transported to his flats skiff in search of tarpon, permit, and bonefish, to gin-clear New Zealand streams where ten-pound brown trout take dry flies, and to offshore Pacific waters locked in battle with 'grander' black marlin. As a bonus, we are allowed entry into Stu's priceless library of experiences on the water with Hall of Fame athletes, legendary authors, captains of industry, and former U.S. Presidents. *My Life in Fishing* is a feast for addicted fly fishermen like me and delightful fare for all anglers. You will heartily enjoy it!"

—CHRISTOPHER J. JORDAN, Executive Vice President, Wells Fargo & Co.

"Besides Stu's vast angling abilities, I've always admired the pride he dedicates to every project. Whether it's a video, book, seminar, TV show, or mixing another of his famous Rum-Dumb-Buggy concoctions, Stu does it with absolute zeal and passion. That's why I'm not surprised that *My Life in Fishing* is an absolute hoot—I've already read it twice!"

—DOUG KELLY, TV, radio, and video producer, travel writer, *Florida Sportsman* magazine contributing editor, IGFA Representative, and author of *Florida's Fishing Legends and Pioneers*

"Grab a drink, kick back, and be ready to be thoroughly entertained by Stu Apte's superb collection of stories from his 50-plus years of guiding and fishing in saltwater."

—BILL KLYN, International Business Development Manager, Patagonia

"Great anglers, and Stu is certainly one of them, have many interesting stories to tell. He has fished such a variety of waters, from the blue seas for sailfish, to the flats for giant tarpon, to Montana's clear trout streams. He has put together what are some of his most interesting stories, and they will delight his readers."

—LEFTY KREH, IGFA Hall of Fame, author of *Fly-Casting Fundamentals*

"What a robust and exhilarating book, which only the inimitable Stu Apte could write because of the amazing life he has lived, the remarkable fishing pals he has had, and his vast fishing experiences. All fly fishers will envy the man, and will hugely enjoy being in a boat with him."

—NICK LYONS, author of *Spring Creek*

"As a driven man, Stu Apte knows no boundaries. He wakes every day with a passionate heart, riveted to be better than he was the day before. His playground is the world, its waters, and the sky above. I was a passenger of Hemingway's and Zane Grey's stories about the virgin waters beyond the reef, over the horizon. Years later Stu Apte refined many of the techniques and tackle used to battle the same fish they wrote about. His high level of success and adventure is stunning, and the bow of his skiff has been sought after by the rich and famous. It was in demand because it was the front-row seat to the new world!

My Life in Fishing is a poignant reminder of what true legends are made of."

—ANDY MILL, Olympian, five-time Gold Cup Champion,
    and author of *A Passion for Tarpon*

"No one knows light tackle, fly, and big fish like Stu Apte. Now he has truly written the book on it. Stu's chapter offering six tips for success catching our watery planet's most sought-after game fish provides all the ammo you'll ever need for success. If stories of angling challenges send your pulse into overdrive as they do mine, *My Life in Fishing* is a must read!"

—SANDY MORET, Founder, Florida Keys Fly Fishing School and
    Florida Keys Outfitters

"Stu Apte is a lot of things to a lot of people, not the least of which is a master storyteller. When reading *My Life in Fishing*, I hear him speaking to me, not us—as he easily entertains, with the corner of his mouth cocked up and an 'Aptini' at the ready. These are yarns of a sport that he treasures, told by a man we dearly love, and it doesn't get any better than this."

—MICHAEL MYATT, Chief Operating Officer, International Game Fish Association

"A book of Stu Apte's memories? Are you kidding me? So many of such memories would be my own and would include or be influenced by him! I consider us all fortunate that a pioneer and raconteur such as Stu should take the time to share so many of the memories that make up this happy book. From ducks to antelope, from brown trout to tarpon, Stu Apte is the real deal and a cherished friend who shares it all in the pages of *My Life in Fishing*."

—FLIP PALLOT, Cofounder, Hell's Bay Boatworks, author, photographer, *Walker's Cay Chronicles* host

"No one has caught more tarpon and billfish on a fly than Stu Apte. No one has been more talented, obsessed, and dedicated in his pursuit. *My Life in Fishing* is his account of a most exciting, lifelong moveable feast among the fish. Enjoy it!"

—JOHN RANDOLPH, Editor/Publisher Emeritus, *Fly Fisherman* magazine, member of the Fly Fishing Hall of Fame

"I first met Stu Apte in the early 1970s when he came to Homosassa to do a story on the newly discovered tarpon fishery there. For me, it was as if God himself had come to visit my home waters—Stu was the icon of American Sportsman Television then, the resident tarpon master. Stu was then and is today the recognized Grand Master of saltwater flats fishing. He puts a lifetime of angling into this book, not only on the flats but on trout streams across the West as well as in blue water pursuits around the world. Stu has been guide and friend to Presidents and celebrities—including Harry Truman, Ernest Hemingway, Ted Williams, Curt Gowdy, Norman Schwarzkopf, and many more, and he preserves in *My Life in Fishing* the memories of many great trips in entertaining detail."

—FRANK SARGEANT, former outdoor editor for the *Tampa Tribune*, editor of *The Fishing Wire,* and author of *The Tarpon Book*

"There is only one Stu Apte—an outstanding angler, pioneering fishing guide, skilled fighter pilot, and experienced airline captain. Every phase of his life has been exciting and memorable. The stories in *My Life in Fishing* reflect adventure and endless memories, and once you read the first one, you won't want to put the book down until you have read them all. These tales were wonderful reading."

—MARK SOSIN, IGFA Hall of Fame, Producer of *Mark Sosin's Saltwater Journal,* and author

"There are many reasons Stu Apte has become an icon in the world of sport fishing. He holds 44 International Game Fish Association records, including some that will never be matched. As an innovator, his major contributions to the development of fishing tackle have set industry standards today. A wonderful storyteller, Stu shares his career highlights with us in these pages. These memorable tales will take you from his adventurous life as jet fighter pilot to master fly fisherman and more. Now you, too, can enjoy great fishing trips with Stu Apte!"

—VIN T. SPARANO, Editor Emeritus, *Outdoor Life* magazine.

"I first met Stu in the 1970s, when *The America Sportsman* and Curt Gowdy brought Stu and his infinite angling wisdom right into my living room. Almost 40 years later, I finally met Stu in person and formed a lasting friendship. Stu has introduced me to CEOs, professional athletes, and other personalities whom I would never have met otherwise. What amazes me is how they welcomed me as a trusted friend based solely on Stu's introduction. To me this speaks volumes about his character and how he has led his life. Yes, Stu's angling knowledge places him on angling's Mount Rushmore, but it's the values he holds in his heart that place him squarely at the epicenter of 'Respected.'"

—BOB STEWART, Executive Producer, *Southwest Florida Outdoors*

"If there is such a thing as an 'ultimate' fishing life, Stu Apte lived it. His clean, crisp telling of his amazing angling adventures in the golden age of fly fishing moves us from being green with envy to being there with him. His stories not only enlarge my own experiences but fill out my bucket list."

—JOAN WULFF, IGFA Hall of Fame, "The First Lady of Fly Fishing," author of *Fly Casting Techniques*

MY LIFE *in* FISHING

Stu Apte

MY LIFE *in* FISHING

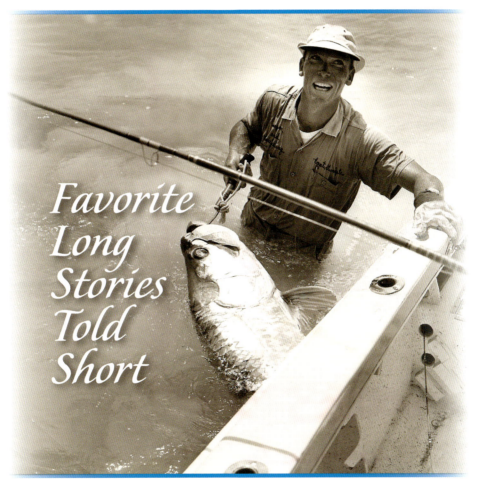

*Favorite
Long
Stories
Told
Short*

STU APTE

Foreword by Thomas McGuane, author of THE LONGEST SILENCE

STONEFLY
PRESS

640 Clematis St. #588
West Palm Beach, FL 33402
FAX: 877-609-3814

For information about discounts on bulk purchases, or
to book the author for an engagement or demonstration,
please contact Stonefly Press at info@stoneflypress.com,
or visit us at Stoneflypress.com.

stoneflypress.com

Printed in the United Sates

20 19 18 17 16   2 3 4 5

Library of Congress Control Number: 2014956695

Stonefly Press

Publisher: Robert D. Clouse

Acquiring Editor: Robert D. Clouse

Copy Editor: Eliani Torres

Proofreading and Indexing: Cape Cod Compositors, Inc.

Photos by Stu and Jeannine Apte except where otherwise indicated.

Contents

Acknowledgments

Sincere thanks to my following friends!

Lamar Underwood, who I'm sure is one of the reasons you will find this selection of short stories a fast and enjoyable read. Thomas McGuane, my sincere thanks to an old fishing friend for writing the Foreword for this book. Pat Ford, great angler and photographer, for the use of some of his fantastic bonefish, barracuda, and cobia photographs. Ian Davis, co-owner of Yellow Dog Fly Fishing Adventures, for the use of a great bonefish release photograph. Steven Bell, for continuing to push me into doing this book. Tom Boyd, my fishing friend who, because of all of his long stories told short, prompted me into even writing this book of short stories.

Stu with a measured 8-foot long monster tarpon on 12-pound class tippet, before its release.

About the Author

STU APTE began his professional career as a Navy fighter pilot during the Korean conflict. He spent the next thirty-four years as a commercial pilot for Pan Am, all the while pursuing his "reel passion" for fishing.

He began fly fishing in the mid-1940s, and began guiding anglers in the Florida Keys in the mid-1950s while laid off from Pan Am. Through the years, Stu has held more than 44 saltwater light tackle and fly rod world records, including the two longest-standing saltwater fly rod records—a 58-pound dolphin caught in 1964 and a 136-pound Pacific sailfish caught in 1965, both on 12-pound tippets.

The Stu Apte Tarpon Fly and the Stu Apte Improved Blood Knot are standard items for most fly fishermen. The Stu Apte Tarpon Fly also has the distinction of being featured on a United States Postal Service stamp in 1991.

In 1969-1970, Stu was inducted into the Fishing Hall of Fame. In 2003, Stu was the recipient of the prestigious Ted Williams Award and in 2004, for the fifth year in a row, was the Pro Celebrity Grand Champion of the Backbone Tournament. Stu had the distinction of joining Ted Williams, Curt Gowdy, Ernest Hemingway, Izaak Walton, and Zane Grey among others when he was inducted into the International Game Fish Association Fishing Hall of Fame on December 11th, 2005. On October 4, 2012, Stu was inducted into the Catskill Fly Fishing Hall of Fame and on April 4, 2013, Stu was honored, along with author Thomas McGuane and actor Michael Keaton, at the 3rd Annual Big Apple Dinner to benefit Bonefish & Tarpon Trust.

As a natural extension of his passion for fly fishing, Stu has written many articles for industry magazines, including *Outdoor Life, Field & Stream,* and *Sports Afield.* He was angling editor of *Sea & Rudder,* a national boating magazine, as well as contributing editor to *Fly Fishing in Salt Waters* magazine, including the back page column, "Down and Dirty with Stu Apte." He was field editor for *Shallow Water Angler,* while also penning the back page column, "Stu Apte on Fishing." He is the author of *Stu Apte's Fishing in the Florida Keys,* and an autobiography, *Of Wind and Tides.*

In addition to writing, Stu has appeared in ABC's *Wide World of Sports,* was field host on ABC's *American Sportsman* TV show , CBS *Sports Spectacular, Thrill-Maker Sports,* ESPN's *On The Fly, Walker Cay Chronicles , Sportsman's Adventures,* the Teddy Award-winning *Sportsman's Journal* with Andy Mill, *"The Legend of Stu Apte",* and ESPN's *Out There* with Trevor Gowdy. Most recently, Stu cohosted *The Outdoor World* TV series on OLN, *Southwest Florida Outdoors* on Fox Sports Network, *Flats Class, Angling Tactics and Techniques* and Ray Van Horn's *Gypsy Angler.*

He directed and starred in a Paramount Studios short subject film *Keys to Fishing Fun,* that premiered in Radio City Music Hall in 1969. He also produced the award-winning *Tarpon Country* film in 1976 and directed the award-winning video series *Saltwater Fly Fishing From A to Z.* His latest video is *Quest for Giant Tarpon,* which won a Teddy Award for best fishing video 1993-1994. He received a 2000 Telly Award for a striped bass episode shot in New England.

Stu is one of the founders and former officer and trustee of the Everglades Protection Association, is a founding father and executive board member of the Bonefish & Tarpon Trust conservation organization, and serves on the advisory board of the International Game Fish Association.

He also had the good fortune of leading the USA/USSR Atlantic salmon exploratory expedition to Russia in 1989.

When Stu is not hosting seminars or attending book signings, he resides in the Florida Keys or Montana with his wife Jeannine, where he writes, photographs, and fishes. Go to www.stuapte.net for more info.

Foreword

Long ago, I was living in the Keys painstakingly learning to fish the flats, channels, and shoals of that still innocent fishery. I had a tide book into which I wrote the discrepancies between Miami tides and all the variations between the Gulf and Atlantic sides and from flat to flat as affected by the channels that wound through or crossed this archipelago. I poled my skiff for days on end trying to find patterns in the things I merely stumbled on. Above all, I tried to pay attention to a few guides on my list of legends—George Hommell, Harry Snow, and Stu Apte. They all had one thing in common: they didn't want you to see what they were doing. Hence, my binoculars. Should you overhear their conversations in the Chat and Chew restaurant on Big Pine, it did little good as they had code names for their secret places.

Apte was the boldest of these, learning and fishing places that had never been fished before, especially in pursuit of tarpon, his specialty. I don't believe anyone has equaled his achievements as a tarpon fisherman: he caught world record fish, he guided others to world records, and he established the ways it would always be done. Others have caught bigger tarpon in the years since, strictly as anglers, guided by others who found the fish. Apte mastered all parts of the puzzle, from exploration and boatmanship to the moment of landing. That stands alone.

At bottom, Apte is an angler, and guiding was his aperture to the rivers and oceans of the world. Fishing with him has been an opportunity for celebrities, athletes, and political figures to raise their game and for Apte to train his own sharp observations on them at the very close range of the inside of a skiff. His impressions of some now-historical figures have a freshness not found elsewhere.

Any reader of this book will pause quite regularly to wonder how Apte fit all this into a life that included a stint as a Navy fighter pilot and a long career flying for Pan American airlines. Apte, still active and fishing, has outlived many of his subjects, including that now-bankrupt airline. I like to imagine that it was his training as a fighter pilot that prepared him to guide and fish in the manner he perfected:

the analysis of conditions with a sharply defined goal. Apte was aggressive, tireless, and purposeful. Just as some boatbuilders don't know how to sail or swim, some guides have little interest in angling beyond their services to their clients. Such is not the case with Apte: few if any of his clients had his own passion for fishing; and it is our good luck that Apte took it to such extremes and allows us here to share his experiences. Let the reader set out with Stu Apte in these pages: the reader will see a lot of country and a lot of water and fish, and will meet some of the century's most interesting people.

—*Thomas McGuane*

Introduction
In the Boat with Stu Apte

Outlined *by a smudge of grayness on the horizon, the docks before us are* like a stage where the lights have not been turned on. The pilings, the shadowy hulks of boats, the satiny sheet of water stretching into the darkness—this is a dramatic and mysterious setting we are approaching. All is quiet, except for the occasional slosh of water against the pilings and the cry of an early rising gull somewhere in the dimness. Despite the stillness, the air feels electric, charged with energy. Every nerve in our bodies makes us live in these moments of excitement and anticipation.

Today we are going fishing with Captain Stu Apte.

Of all the guides and anglers who have ever leaned on a pushpole on the flats of the Florida Keys, Stu Apte stands out like an icon. To fish with him is like opening a vault of 50 years of experiences and observations—all of which are going to make your day on the water not only more successful, but more enduring and meaningful as well. You'll see things you'll never forget.

Perhaps you feel as if you've already been fishing with Stu Apte, even though you've never been in the boat with him. There are DVDs and films aplenty, in various formats, television programs—some new, some from historic archives—and magazine articles, with Stu's images frozen on the printed page. And there is his autobiography, his memoir, the book *Of Wind and Tides*.

As a former editor of both *Sports Afield* and *Outdoor Life* and several anthologies, I have devoted my professional life to the fishing and hunting in print. One of the parts of that experience I have treasured most was the opportunity to put Stu Apte on the printed page.

This collection of Stu Apte stories has the range of the Pan Am jets he once captained—from the Florida Keys to the Great Barrier Reefs in the land "Down Under" to the bright rivers of the Emerald Isle. With many other stops along the way.

It has tarpon in epic battles on the flats; all the flats-fishing favorites from barracudas to bonefish and permit; tidewater favorites like snook and redfish; monster shark encounters; a search for 2,000-pound marlin; and proven techniques on everything from fighting fish to rigging a shrimp for bait. Stu's passion for angling extends far beyond the salt, and his stories about matching hatches for rising trout, or teasing lunker bass from their lairs, or meeting the salmon runs make entertaining and informative side trips in this collection.

Print man that I am, I still have more sense than to try to tell you that the fishing in print is as good as the real thing. Even so, I heartily urge you to go fishing with Stu Apte in these pages. He might take you into some waters that are familiar to you. Often, I guarantee you, he will take you beyond anything you have ever known.

God, how I wish I could go fishing with Stu Apte today. Really fishing, out on the flats.

But I can't. This book is as close as I can come to that experience.

I'll take it. And, by the way, I'm warning people not to ask to borrow my copy.

—*Lamar Underwood*

LAMAR UNDERWOOD is the former editor-in-chief of both *Outdoor Life* and *Sports Afield*. He has edited many anthologies, including *The Greatest Fishing Stories Ever Told* and *Into the Backing*. His most recent fishing book is *1001 Fishing Tips*.

chapter 1

You Won't Believe It!

But try anyway. Because this really happened!

At daybreak, I had my skiff in position on an ocean-side flat with a white sand bottom, a mere 12-minute run from my house on Plantation Key. I had fished there the day before and pretty well knew the tarpons' traveling pattern during this phase of the incoming tide.

The run out had been a familiar one, through many shortcuts in the black dark. I wanted to be first boat, in the best position when the sun started peeking over the horizon and the strings of big tarpon came swimming by.

It was an almost flat-calm morning with the slightest breeze coming from behind us as I tied the skiff in a spot that would give my novice angler the best shots possible.

I could already see a few tarpon rolling in the distance, heading our way. Everything was falling into place for what I wanted to be a very special great day.

With me was Bert Scherb, a true conservationist, especially when it pertains to bonefish and tarpon. He's also an outstanding fly fisherman and a good friend.

Back in the late 1970s and the 1980s, I was first vice president of the Everglades Protection Association (EPA), a conservation organization in South Florida with a mission statement trying to limit the commercial fishing in the Everglades National Park. Bert invited me to his home in Chicago, Illinois, to put on a slide show in order to try to raise some funds for the EPA. He had invited around 30 "high rollers" who liked to fish to a fund-raising cocktail party. We did raise quite a few thousands of dollars that night!

Now fast-forwarding to only a few years ago, Bert called me and said he had a wealthy gentleman from Chicago (we'll call him "John") who would make a sizable donation to Bonefish Tarpon Trust (BTT) if I would take him fly fishing for his first-ever tarpon. As one of BTT's founders and a member of the executive board, I was always extremely happy to do whatever was necessary to raise funds for our extensive research programs. BTT's mission statement says it all:

> To conserve and enhance global bonefish, tarpon and permit fisheries and their environments through stewardship, research, education and advocacy . . .

The list goes on, with objectives critical to both anglers and guides who are dedicated to preserving and maintaining our fishing opportunities.

I picked a day during what I consider to be prime tides for the early tarpon migration heading down the Florida Keys toward Key West. Bert told me his friend was only a mediocre trout fly fisherman and had never cast a fly to a tarpon. With that information, I knew I had to pick a place where the tarpon would be easy to see and easy to cast to. There are a few places in the Upper Florida Keys that fit the bill, but you have to get to those sites early before anyone else does.

So I asked them to be at my house on Plantation Key at 5:30, a half hour before daybreak. I had already lowered my skiff into the water and loaded all the equipment necessary, including food and drinks, on board by the time they arrived.

Now that we had accomplished my first goal—setting up before other guides pulled into the spot—it was important for me to get John ready for action. I had him on the casting platform before the tarpon were in range, stripping the proper amount of fly line off the reel and stretching it so that when he made a cast, it would come up off the deck and go through the rod guides smoothly. The night before, I had cleaned and dressed the 11-weight fly line and selected the flies I'd previously had success with in this particular area. We should be ready! And, there should be no mistakes!

To say that John was only a mediocre fly fishing person would be very kind to him. He had a typical beginner's problem of not waiting for his backcast to get fully behind him. He started the forward cast too soon, which meant he had to compensate by pushing his arm and rod forward. That opened up his loop and basically destroyed his forward cast.

I thought it was most important to get John casting correctly, so we ignored the first group of fish that came streaming by the boat. He did have good natural coordination and timing and seemed to understand what I was telling and showing him. His casting quickly improved.

Now, if he could repeat that type of cast when he saw the fish—without the "buck fever" that strikes so many tarpon fly fishermen—we would be in business.

John managed to get the fly in front of, and briefly hook, five different big tarpon, with only two of them hooked long enough to get into his backing. Setting the hook in the hard mouth of a big tarpon is not an easy thing to do, especially if you are a newcomer in this game. Sometimes lady luck can be a rewarding factor.

About an hour after we got started, another boat pulled up about 300 yards behind us, on another big stretch of white sand bottom. He should've been getting some shots at tarpon that bypassed us and at some of the tarpon that came by wide of us. He was not creating a problem for us, so I did not pay any heed. I was really too busy helping John to see the fish and cast the fly into the correct area for properly intercepting the swimming fish.

Evidently, the guy in this other boat was not getting the amount of tarpon flow he wanted and was tired of seeing John hooking so many fish. He pulled up his anchor, fired up his outboard, and motored outside of us into the deeper water until he was a short distance in front of us. He then swung directly in front of my boat and dropped his anchor, cutting off the flow of our fish. He was close enough that I could have cast a fly into his boat.

I had never seen this happen before in such a blatant way.

Bert and John both looked at me with wonder in their eyes, and Bert said, "I can't believe I saw what I just witnessed! This guy committed one of the cardinal sins of the flats by coming directly in front of our boat and cutting your fish off."

As I was pulling up my anchor, I quickly told Bert and John that I was going to pole up to this so-called gentleman, who had a young teenager in the boat fishing with him, possibly his son, and nicely explain the basic flats "rules of the road" to him.

Holding my boat directly alongside his boat with my pushpole, I politely said, "Excuse me, sir, but your pulling up in front of me like you just did is considered a cardinal sin while flats fishing here in the Florida Keys. I got up very early to be in this position before anyone else. Now you have come along and cut me off from the flow of fish."

He responded in a somewhat belligerent tone, saying, "I have fished the Keys with quite a number of different backcountry guides, and they all do this!"

"Oh, yeah?" I replied. "Which guides have you fished with who did something like this?"

"I can't think of their names right now," he shouted, "but they all do it!"

"Well, my friend," I called, "I have been fishing and living in the Florida Keys for sixty years, and I don't believe you are telling the truth. Furthermore, you are not showing this young man the proper way to behave."

"Who in the hell do you think you are? Stu Apte?"

"Sir, that is *exactly* who I am!"

Without another word, he fired his engine, pulled his anchor, and idled a long way into the deep water before jumping his boat up on the plane and leaving the area.

Believe it or not, it really happened.

Stu Apte, young Naval Aviator, readies to go aboard
an aircraft carrier for his first landings.

chapter 2

How to Worry Your Mom

*How my flats boat got its name. The story has a
happy ending, but in fact, it almost killed me.*

Follow along with me, in the cockpit of my navy fighter jet, the F9F-5 Panther.
The time is late August 1954.

We have been flying a rocket and bomb practice exercise. Today has been a good
shoot, and I am feeling pretty confident about my ability to hit the bull's-
eye with both rockets and bombs. I climb to 20,000 feet and head back to NAAS
Oceana, near Norfolk, with my wingman.

The air is smooth, and I am almost fully relaxed, looking off to my left at the North
Carolina–Virginia coastline. My thoughts briefly stray to a fishing trip I took not too
long ago, looking for big, 100-pound tarpon. Every summer, these fish migrate along
this coast, as far north as Chesapeake Bay. As for my favorite fish to catch in my home
state of Florida—it has always been tarpon.

Staring out the window of the cockpit, it looks like a calm morning along the
beach—perfect conditions for catching my favorite fish.

This picture disappears in a blink.

With a start, I am brought back to reality as two fire-warning lights flash and glare
at me in the cockpit. In this model Panther jet, the emergency instruction to all pilots
is: "If a fire-warning light comes on in the plenum chamber, eject. Eject immediately! The aircraft is going to blow up." The plenum is where fuel and air combine in a
potentially explosive mixture.

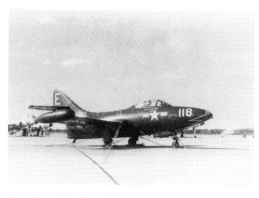

Stu piloted the Navy's F9-F-5 Panther fighter jet on the mission that almost cost his life.

Damn, two fire-warning lights have come on, and one of them is in the plenum chamber.

The ejection procedure words to remember in the F9F-5 Panther jets are, PRE–POS–OX–PULL.

PRE: Activate your **pre**-ejection lever on the right side of the cockpit, which arms the ejection seat and jettisons the canopy. POS: **Position** your feet in the stirrups of the ejection seat to prevent your kneecaps from being painfully removed as you exit the airplane. OX: Reach down and activate your bailout **oxygen** bottle in your parachute seat by pulling a tab in the seat portion of your parachute. PULL: Reach up, grab, and smartly **pull** down the two rungs extending from the ejection seat that houses the face curtain, in order to fire the seat. (The navy believes that the face curtain will give the pilot some protection when he hits the high-velocity air stream.)

Although I can say "Pre–Pos–Ox–Pull" faster than I can complete the procedure, for this run-though, I definitely set a record.

When the airplane explodes in a massive fireball, I am already on my way out. My wingman barely misses me in his evasive maneuver to avoid hitting my airplane's debris, and probably me along with it. The last thing I recall is pulling my face curtain. I don't remember tumbling through the air, unbuckling my seat belt and shoulder harness, or kicking myself out of the seat and pulling the rip cord.

My wingman sees the parachute open and broadcasts a Mayday on the Guard Channel, which everyone monitors. The naval air station's job is to immediately dispatch a rescue helicopter.

As I float toward the Atlantic Ocean from 20,000 feet, I drift in and out of consciousness until my mind actually flashes back quite vividly to when I was five years old. We're living in a house on the corner of Southwest Fourth Street and 13th Avenue, in Miami. Because I was just a little tyke, my next-door neighbor's goldfish pond is full of what, it seems to me, are monster-size fish. I was using some of my mother's sewing thread, a straight pin that I bent to form a hook, and some dough balls to form a makeshift fishing apparatus.

The next thing I remember is waking up in the Portsmouth Naval Hospital, some 40 hours later. When those hours are recalled for me secondhand, they tell me that luckily the dispatched helicopter was hovering nearby as I hit the water. The pilot of the helicopter immediately dispatched a paramedic into the water, who pulled the toggle switch on my Mae West to inflate it. The paramedic also disconnected the parachute, untangling me from the shroud lines.

At the hospital, when I felt stable enough to make a phone call, my father uttered an expression that was to stay with me all my life: "Mom's Worry." He said, "Stu, I want you to know that you really are your mom's worry." From that time on, all my boats and my radio "handle" have been *Mom's Worry.*

I am released from the hospital with a few stitches in my head from some of the debris, a strangulated hernia, and numerous cuts and bruises—all injuries that will remind me of this adventure for the rest of my life. I looked like I had been in one helluva fight. After such a close call, I felt like God was telling me that life—and fishing—should mean a whole lot more to me. I have spent my life since that time letting my adventures fulfill that prophecy.

Spinning tackle is perfect for Snook in the backcountry.
This beauty hit a jig. *Photo by Capt. Dave Denkert*

chapter 3

Fishing's Flat-Out Best

On the thin-water flats, where the tides push
and pull and you can see what you're hunting,
sport fishing's finest hours await.

"What is your favorite place to fish?"

I've answered that question at least a thousand times, and the answer is always the same: Of all the places I have fished in this world—every continent except Antarctica—fishing the flats of the Florida Keys is as good as it gets.

My credentials for that declaration start with the fact that I have been fishing the South Florida flats since the 1940s. These areas of thin water, with depths depending upon the tides, range from a few hundred yards wide to several miles, and they include a good portion of Florida Bay. There, I am at home. There, I can fish in a variety of ways for many types of powerful, fast, and interesting fish that will test my skill and my tackle. I can't think of a better way to spend the fishing days I am blessed to enjoy.

Sure, there's always a newfound faraway hot spot somewhere in the world that grabs my attention, makes me want to book a trip. Probably the fish there have not been disturbed by anglers and outboard motors, and they're much easier to stalk and catch. And sometimes it's the fish themselves that make me want to go—worthy battlers that I admire like Atlantic salmon, trout of many types, striped bass.

But always I return home to the flats.

Trust me, I am far from being alone in my passion for this type of fishing.

Stu designs his own special jigs for enticing nice backcountry snook like this beauty. *Photo by Capt. Dave Denkert*

Day in and day out, weather permitting, with proper knowledge and skills sharpened, a reasonably good angler can catch all the many species that roam the shallow flats of South Florida.

The silver king tarpon is definitely my favorite, but not far behind are snook, bonefish, permit, redfish, barracudas, trout, lady fish, and jack crevalle. I'll not leave out the opportunity to do battle with a variety of big and small sharks. Lemon, blacktip, bonnethead, tiger, and bull sharks can all make for an exciting day when the other fishing is slow.

My wife, Jeannine, likes to tell her nonfishing friends that a trip onto the flats is a trip for sights and sounds that you cannot see elsewhere. Looking into the water, you can look into a secret world of crabs, stingrays, leopard stingrays, starfish, loggerhead sponges, sharks, and porpoises to name a few resident creatures. Overhead, or in nearby shallows, you'll see egrets, bald eagles, ospreys, laughing terns, roseate spoonbills, and—yes—some brightly colored flamingos. The world around you and literally beneath your feet is filled with sound and color and the movements of great fish in the throbbing currents.

Jeannine is right: There's nothing like being on the flats, whether the fish are biting or not.

Gearing up for enjoying the world of the flats begins with wearing polarized sunglasses to cut the glare from the surface of the water so you can see past it to the bottom. To have the most sport from your fishing, I suggest using a 7-foot medium-light spinning outfit—or a bait-casting outfit, if that's your cup of tea. There are a variety of baits to use for most fish, starting with live shrimps, live silver-dollar-size crabs; a variety of jigs, varying from ⅛-ounce to ⅜-ounce in weight, sometimes fishing them pure and other times tipping them with a piece of shrimp when the fish are being persnickety and acting tough.

The weather and the tides are the two things that can make or break your day's fishing on the flats. During our winter months, a passing cold front might drop our water temperatures into the low 60s (Fahrenheit). The cold conditions can lead to blank days for many anglers, even in Florida, but I have favorite ways to cope.

I can still catch bonefish and, yes, tarpon because I know where and when they will be in different areas. For bonefish, I look for a morning incoming tide on the ocean side, with a late-afternoon outgoing tide that carries the now-warmed-up water off the shallow flats to the deep. That will generally get the bonefish pushing into the warmer water to feed.

A similar scenario works when tarpon fishing in the backcountry. There are a number of large flats bordering the Gulf of Mexico—like the Nine-Mile Bank. The water on the down current side of a large bank late in the afternoon will be the warmest water around the area and should suck whatever tarpon are in the area into it.

Extremely hot weather presents the other side of the water-temperature issue. It can be a challenge.

During the end of last August, I was scheduled to shoot a TV show for *Southwestern Florida Outdoors*. It was a one-day shoot of mixed bag fishing with my wife,

Using bait-casting tackle with his own special jig,
Stu landed and released this Goliath grouper.

Above. With nice weather, the drama of flats fishing plays out on a beautiful stage, where fish are visible in the thin water as they move and feed with the tides. *Photo by Pat Ford*

This Goliath grouper is small, but a worthy game fish.

Backcountry coves are home for birds like the great white heron.

Jeannine, being the on-camera star for her first time. The temperature was in the 90s and we were sitting right in the middle of a high barometer, creating some extremely low tides. Our guide was my friend Capt. Dave Denkert, one of the good guys who makes sure everybody has a good time, even if the fishing is slow.

We left the dock at 7 A.M. and made the 40-minute run to Flamingo, where Dave had us rigged with live pinfish. We cast them into a deep trough near one of the islands, looking for a big snook. We got there just at the last of the incoming tide and hooked and lost a couple of snook and landed a couple of Goliath groupers before the tide turned and started ripping outbound with gusto.

By ten o'clock, the water temperature had risen to 90 degrees and some of the surrounding flats were starting to go dry. As had our fishing!

Dave made a command decision. He said, "Okay. Wind them in, we've got to get out of here before it's too late. I think I know where we have to go."

Twenty minutes later, we were on the edge of a vast flat by the deepest part of Snakebite Channel. The tide was rushing out, leaving most of the banks barely awash, and the water was slightly milky from muddying mullet, signifying good conditions.

My first cast up current and slightly across the channel with a ¼-ounce bucktail jig produced an immediate hit shortly after I let it sink to the bottom. I brought in a 20-inch snook. Jeannine's first cast with a ⅜-ounce jig tipped with a piece of shrimp netted her a catfish, which of course did not make her a happy camper.

She came up with a nice snook on her next cast into the same area. And we had fast fishing for the next couple of hours, landing a total of 27 snook, 3 redfish, 5 catfish, all too many ladyfish and jack crevalle, making for a bang-up mixed bag TV show.

A big lemon shark provided an exciting ending by grabbing a 30-inch snook close enough to the boat that the cameraman was so busy getting out of its way, he completely missed the shot.

Weather, tides, characteristics of the different flats, habits of the fish—it's all part of flats fishing. Obviously, there's a lot to learn if you're going to be successful. To me, it's just as obvious that the rewards will be worth the effort.

Stu straining to heft this 151-pound tarpon—then the largest fish ever caught
on fly-fishing tackle, and a world record for 12-pound-test tippet.

chapter 4

Record Tarpon: The Challenge and the Prize

*Your tackle, the conditions, the man on the pushpole, your
casting ability . . . get all that right, and you still need a
lot of luck when record tarpon are in your sights.*

Even though a fresh wind from the south had spread a glistening chop across
the water's surface, through polarized glasses I spotted a school of about 40 fish
traveling in our direction.

 t first they were only faint wavering shadows, but instinct told me they were
tarpon, probably of good size.

"Be ready to cast at ten o'clock," I instructed Guy Valdene, who stood in the stern
of the boat.

"Ready," he answered.

As soon as the lead fish were in range, my companion false cast once and placed
the orange-and-yellow streamer fly a little off target. Just the same, a very big fish
turned out of the school and came after it. I held my breath, waiting for the strike
that I knew would be more like an explosion.

But in his excitement—and from inexperience also, I suppose—Guy struck too
soon and took the fly away from the big open mouth.

"Cast it back again!" I shouted. This time the fly fell closer to the tail end of the
school, and instantly a small fish had it. In the same split second, it was up and out

Note: This article was written in 1967, when I was 37 years old, living and guiding in the Florida Keys
and also flying for Pan Am. The records cited are accurate for that particular time.

of the water in the kind of jump that never fails to make the bristles stand up on the back of my neck.

"Bow!" I shouted. "Bow from your waist and thrust the rod toward the fish, giving it some slack every time he jumps."

What followed was a typically wild and watery contest, which only the silver king can provide. The fish seemed to jump in two places at once, and I had a busy time poling the boat to keep Guy in the fight. He did a pretty good job, too, because 30 minutes later he had maneuvered the tarpon into position for gaffing. I jammed the pushpole into the bottom, lashed the boat rope to the pole, and grabbed my lip gaff. On the first attempt, I put the release gaff into its lower jaw, and that's when all hell broke loose.

"I am never happier than when I'm
prospecting the Florida Keys flats
for tarpon, fly rod in hand."

For several seconds, the tarpon shook its head crazily while I just held on. That was enough to shear off the metal part of the gaff, which had rusted nearly through, unseen, inside the wooden handle. So I had to boat, unhook, and release the fish, a 60-pounder, with my bare hands alone. When I was finished, my fingers were raw and bleeding. But what a happy scene it was.

"Congratulations," I said to my companion, over and over, because it was his first tarpon on any tackle and the largest fish he had ever taken in a short career of fly rodding. It was also the first fish in an uncommonly unsuccessful fishing trip to the Lower Florida Keys that had started weeks before.

"Now the jinx is broken," Guy laughed, "and the pressure is off. Now you take the rod and cast to the next tarpon we see. What I need is a chance to rest and unwind."

That was an unusual offer, since Guy was the client and I was the guide.

After splitting a cold beer, I picked up the rod, checked the leader for fraying, and stood ready to cast. At that moment, I had no idea one of the greatest fishing experiences of my life was soon to begin. Out of the corner of my eye, I saw tailing tarpon coming our way.

But that is getting ahead of my story.

Fishing has always been the greatest thing in my life. In fact, it is my life—I am never happier than when I'm prospecting the Florida Keys flats for tarpon, fly rod in hand. Developing new and better tackle is another special interest of mine.

Luckily, I live in the Florida Keys, where fishing is always excellent and nearby. It is also an area where light tackle angling for big fish had produced a whole new cult of outdoorsmen.

I grew up in Miami and remember my first childhood fishing trip, in my next-door neighbor's goldfish pond. I also recall getting up at four o'clock on many mornings and bicycling to Biscayne Bay near the present site of Rickenbacker Causeway. There, I squeezed in a few hours of fishing before school. Nowadays at 36, I often do the same thing before or after one of my flights as copilot with Pan Am.

In 1942, at the age of 12, I became infected with the light-tackle bug when I acquired an old bamboo casting rod and a freshwater plug-casting reel. With it, I landed my first tarpon, a 15-pounder, but broke the tip of the rod when it was caught in the spokes of my bike one morning. That was a blow. Not much later, I earned enough money for my first used fly rod, and I was hooked for keeps. Homer Rhode Jr., then a game warden and a well-known fisherman, taught me how to tie flies for saltwater fish. In 1949, I caught my first tarpon on a fly—a 20-pounder. A few months later, I landed my first really big tarpon, a 96½-pounder, but it was taken on a plug near Marco Island, on the southwest cost of Florida. It seems like I always had a rod of some kind in my hands in those days.

But fishing had to wait for the Korean Conflict, when I enlisted in the navy as an aviation cadet and went into flight training. After graduation, I flew F9F Panther jets, FJ-3 Furies, and the Delta Wing F7U-3 Cutlass from the decks of various aircraft carriers. All the while, I dreamed of fishing at home, and only a few days after release from active duty, I caught my first fly rod tarpon weighing over 100 pounds. It was the greatest possible way to celebrate being a civilian again.

With all the flying experience, it was only natural to seek and obtain a pilot's job with Pan American World Airways. But lacking seniority in the early days with the airline, I was subject to frequent, long layoffs. During the downtime, I began to guide winter tourists from my headquarters at Little Torch Key, 28 miles north of Key West. The truth is that I flew very little for several years and became a full-time guide. It was a very meager beginning, however, because my first guide boat was borrowed from a friend, Bill Curtis, who is an immensely successful guide today. Because I enjoyed both the sport and the work so much, I had considerable success. I would fish from daybreak to dusk if the customer was willing. As a result, I built up a clientele of expert, serious fishermen who still fish with me today—as friends.

Luckily, I guess, my customers began catching more than their share of prizes and citations in the Metropolitan Miami and other Florida fishing tournaments. At the same time, I gradually became more of a specialist in fly rodding and I concentrated more and more on fly fishing for tarpon. I consider them just about the most exciting and unpredictable of all our game species. They're big, they're strong, and they're highly acrobatic. In addition, the big ones were very available where I was guiding.

Some good breaks came my way—such as guiding jobs in motion pictures and in a two-day tarpon fishing contest for experts that was filmed as an *ABC's Wide*

Staking out by tying the skiff to the pushpole is an excellent way to ambush traveling tarpon. . .once you have found their traveling area! Here Stu and friend Capt. Herb Pontin get *Mom's Worry* set for action.

World of Sports fly fishing spectacular. In that production, I handled the boat for Joe Brooks—angling writer, authority, and friend—who easily won the fly rod tarpon competition. Two years earlier, I had been guiding Joe when he caught the world record tarpon on a fly rod. It weighed 148½ pounds and pulled me into the water twice when I gaffed it. That catch was the most thrilling fishing experience I had ever known. (That tarpon adventure is told in full in this book in chapter 11.)

I had a hand in other records. I was guiding Kay Brodney, a librarian in our Library of Congress, when she caught her 137½-pounder, which remains the women's fly rod tarpon record.

Twice Ray Donnersberger, a Chicago businessman, was fishing with me when he captured the best fly rod tarpon in the Metropolitan Miami Fishing Tournament. And I guided Russ Ball of Bryn Mawr, Pennsylvania, when he caught the world record tarpon of 170½ pounds on spinning tackle using 8-pound-test line. Although I had little opportunity to fish myself during those busy years of full-time guiding, I did catch the largest tarpon at that time ever caught by a guide on his own. It weighed 132½ pounds. Mark Sosin of New Jersey was handling the boat for me that day.

To qualify for a saltwater fly rod record, the catch must conform to certain rules and regulations. These parameters are observed by all major fishing clubs and tournaments and have recently been given official continent-wide status by the Saltwater Fly-Rodders of America, the international custodian of the records. The fly rod can be no shorter than 6 feet and no longer than 10 feet. The fly must be cast in the orthodox manner of fly fishing, not trolled or drifted. The fish must be fairly hooked, fought, and brought to gaff or net without the aid of another person, except to handle the boat or the landing device.

No doubt the most important regulation for a record is that the leader cannot test more than 12 pounds, although a shock tippet of any strength may be used, because of the sharp teeth and gill plates of many saltwater species. Very recently, the Saltwater Fly-Rodders have added other tippet classes of 6-, 10-, and 15-pound-test.

Russ Ball, left, and a young Capt. Stu Apte, right, with Russ's 170½-pound world record tarpon on 12-pound-test line.

The outfit that I am using includes a 9-foot, medium-action, 5⅓-ounce fly rod with oversize snake guides; a carb-aloy tip-top; and a thin fore grip above the main grip to help in holding the rod when playing big fish. The large snake guides permit better shooting of the large (WF11F) tapered lines I use. The most unique feature of the rod is a 4½-foot insert that I helped to develop. This fits into (or inside) the rod's butt section after the fish is hooked and gives extra backbone against the struggle of a really big fish. However, it would interfere with casting if inserted before the fish is hooked.

My reel is a single-action, positive retrieve with capacity for 200 yards of 27-pound-test backing, plus the 30 yards of WF11F fly line. The butt section of my leader is 6 feet of 30- or 40-pound-test monofilament joined to the fly line with a nail knot covered with Pliobond, a plastic coating. To meet fly rodding regulations, my middle section of leader is at least 18 inches of 12-pound-test monofilament. Beyond that, I use 12 inches (the maximum permitted) of 100-pound-test monofilament as a shock tippet. The three sections are joined by the Stu Apte improved blood knot, which I developed when testing lines for the Stren division of the DuPont Corporation. This is an excellent all-around outfit for fly rodding the salt.

With it, or with something very similar, I have set world records for dolphin (58 pounds), jack crevalle (24 pounds), Pacific sailfish (136 pounds), and yellowfin tuna (28 pounds). All these were set during two trips to Panama.

It was only natural that I should start thinking seriously, perhaps too seriously, about catching some records right in my own backyard. The fly rod tarpon record, for instance.

For one thing, where I lived, the intense spirit of competition was always present. Such expert fishermen, members of the prestigious Miami Beach Rod and Reel Club, as Luke Gorham, Al Pfleuger Jr., Lee Cuddy, and Bart Foth were constantly out to set new records in South Florida waters.

But I had something far more important than that spurring me on: I knew that there were a number of tarpon in the Lower Keys much larger than any ever taken before. I had seen them many times, and on a number of occasions had seen them hooked. So had most of the other tarpon guides. Just the year before, for example, a customer of guide George Hommell, Jr. hooked a tarpon larger than 200 pounds on a fly rod; Hommell actually had it on the gaff, but it broke free. "I have no doubt whatsoever," the veteran guide remarked later, "that soon someone will land a two-hundred-plus-pounder on a fly."

In 1962, I had come close to it myself. The camera crew of a national TV network was filming a tarpon movie near Big Pine Key, and I spent a couple of days casting for tarpon to give them some fill-in jump shots. One of the fish I hooked, looked to be 185 pounds, absolute minimum. I held on to it for several jumps, but the line wrapped around the reel handle, and the 12-pound leader snapped.

I remember other fish of similar size being hooked—and lost. The day before Joe Brooks got his 148½-pound fly rod record, I was poling for Dave Newell when he hooked and nearly boated a fish in the 170- to 180-pound class. There must have been an unusual invasion of huge tarpon at that time because only a few days later, I was guiding Lee Cuddy, a Miami tackle dealer, when he also tied into an extraordinary fish of at least 180 pounds, and probably much more.

It would be impossible to forget that occasion. The fish struck an orange-and-yellow streamer near Coupon Bight, and after a two-hour fight joined up with a passing school of tarpon and actually led the school out to deep water. First it passed through Newfound Harbor Channel, and from there we followed it through Hawk Channel to the edge of the Gulf Stream between Looe Key and American Reef Light, a total distance of about seven miles. Once, a hammerhead shark made a pass at the tarpon but unaccountably turned away. At times we were close enough to the fish to see the orange-and-yellow fly in its jaw. When the fish finally broke off after 5 hours and 15 minutes of pressure, Lee had tears in his eyes. I don't blame him, because so did I.

In 1964, I came within an eyelash of gaffing a 200-pounder for sure. The fish was hooked by Ray Donnersberger in a place I would rather not identify, but which I now call Monster Point. After taking Ray's fly, the fish ran into very shallow rocky water, where it began to jump crazily. It seemed to go berserk. This was one time I believed the fish was badly hurt by jumping and falling back on the rocks, because it began spewing blood in all directions until the water was amber colored.

After one wild jump landed almost beside the boat, I reached for the gaff. But then the 12-pound-test leader slipped under the gill plate and was cut. The fish swam away, slowly and weakly.

Two years later, in 1966, I was guiding Mark Sosin and Leon Martuch (of Scientific Anglers) around Sugarloaf Key. As luck would have it, the first tarpon Leon had ever hooked—in fact, the first he had ever seen—was in the 175-pound category. He did an excellent job of playing it, but after an hour or so, the fish broke off. Had the day not been abnormally rough and windy, I believe we could have boated that fish.

Perhaps I shouldn't go any further, because these next items may seem impossible. Anyhow, the Russ Ball 170½-pounder, which is still the spinning record, was the smallest fish in a school of about 20.

And in 1963, I saw a tarpon that was much closer to 300 than to 250 pounds. Yes, you read that right: 300 pounds! It was by far the biggest I have ever seen in or out of the water anywhere.

That morning I was guiding Sam Clark, a Washington, D.C., attorney and an experienced salmon fisherman. We were fishing the ocean side of Sugarloaf Key when the monster inhaled Sam's fly. It made just one jump, close enough at 30 feet so that we had a good clear look at it. Sam was so shaken that he froze on the reel, and of course, the 12-pound leader snapped.

So it isn't any wonder that I have seriously started thinking about a record of my own. For the last couple of years, I have reserved the best periods—which I call the prime tarpon tides—for that purpose. These tides come during the new and full moons of March, April, May, and sometimes June in the Lower Florida Keys, as long as the water is warm enough (74 degrees or more) and the wind less than 10 knots. I base those conditions on my own experience in the past 15 years. But let me explain why these are not the only times when tarpon fishing is productive.

In February of this year, with a few days off from flying, I flew over to Deep Water Cay in the Bahamas with my wife, Bernice, mostly to relax and for a change of pace. One evening we were fly fishing a shallow flat for mutton snappers when we met another angler doing the same thing with unusually good skill and coordination. He introduced himself as Guy Valdene of Palm Beach, and we began a fortunate friendship.

That evening we spent several hours discussing fly rodding in the salt—and especially for tarpon. The upshot was that I agreed to guide him for tarpon during the full moon tides of March and April. It didn't work out very well, at least not at first, during March. The winds, which were seldom less than 25 knots, nearly blew us off the flats. And it was very cold. It reminded me exactly of the spring tide periods a year before, which I spent record hunting with guide Russ Gray and old friend Erwin Bauer, who is an adventure writer and the editor of *The Saltwater Fisherman's Bible.*

As had happened to me in 1966, Guy and I did hook some fish in spite of the weather, but nothing of any consequence. It takes far more than unfavorable weather to discourage me. Luckily, Guy was a kindred spirit, and we were back in the Keys to fish the new moon tides in early April as planned. For the first couple of days, the weather was considerably better, but tarpon had not yet moved onto the flats in big numbers. Still, Guy had about 50 chances to present flies to tarpon, and he briefly hooked several. I believe that two of them would have been good enough to break the existing fly rod record. But no fish of any size were landed by the time the weather deteriorated.

Once more, the fishing ranged from unpleasant to almost impossible. "I'm still game," I said while driving back to Miami.

"Count me in," Guy replied.

That's how that April full moon found us back in the Lower Keys.

On the second day of fishing, we began to encounter large numbers of tarpon, and it was on a flat that I code-named the Bullfighters that Guy broke the ice when I boated and released his first tarpon—the 60-pounder described in the opening of this chapter. A few moments later, I stood in the stern, fly rod in hand, hoping to catch another—only much, much larger.

I didn't have long to wait. The boat drifted very slowly for a short distance when I spotted a school of 40 or 50 fish cruising just out of casting range. The water was calm and I knew they would be spooky, so I crouched down low to cut the size of my silhouette against the sky. From that position, I waited for them to come within casting distance. The fish leading the school was a large one, but there was a much bigger tarpon near the center of the school. Still, I decided to make my presentation to the first fish, rather than risk having my line fall across other tarpon to reach the largest, and thereby spook all of them. Now, I felt the same surge of excitement and suspense I always feel when big tarpon are the targets.

I cast my yellow-and-orange saddle-hackle streamer in the path of the pack, allowed it to settle. As the fish approached, I began the retrieve. The leader charged after it for about 10 feet, then started to turn away. I stopped the fly, butterflies in my stomach.

The tarpon came back. I twitched the fly and the fish had it. I set the hook instinctively. And I could feel the tarpon react all the way down to my heels.

The first run was short, interrupted by two jumps, and did not even strip off the 30 yards of fly line and get into my backing. I figured the fish between 115 and 120 pounds—good trophy size, but not the record fish I am always thinking about. After that initial run, I even turned to Guy and suggested that he take the rod and fight the fish just for the practice.

"No thanks," he answered. "I'll just relax and watch the pro."

Although I didn't know it at the time, Guy's reply was the second-biggest break of the whole trip for me. His earlier suggestion that I cast while he poled the boat was the first.

After the fish's first short run, my companion had to pole in earnest. The second run was longer and included two more jumps. But thanks to the combination of Guy's poling and my pumping for all the tackle would stand, I worked the tarpon in close to the boat, where it made a head-shak-

Stu and Guy Valdene at the scale.

ing half lurch out of the water. Mentally, I revised its weight upward to about 130 pounds or slightly more.

At that point, the tarpon had been hooked ten minutes and if Guy had been fishing, I would have made my move with the gaff. Probably I would have connected because my record at boating fish is good.

The leader was through the tip-top of the fly rod.

But something happened. The fish spooked—and began a screaming run. No bonefish I have ever hooked ran any faster. There was no stopping it or even slowing it down.

First Guy tried to keep up with the mad dash by poling, but no soap, so we decided to start the outboard. To do so quickly became the most urgent thing on earth, because for the first time since I had filled the fly reel four years before, I could see the metal spool through the last windings of backing. Somehow, I got the outboard tilted down into position and the drag adjusted on the reel, but the rapid acceleration of the motor almost tossed me overboard.

And because the boat was heading in the right direction, there were 20 feet of slack line in the water and the fish had dead-ended its run into a tiny mangrove island.

"Neutral, put the motor in neutral!" I shouted. As I reeled frantically to regain lost line.

Since the strong tidal current was flowing past the island, I wasn't sure if I was hooked to the tarpon or to the mangroves. And since I still was not thinking of this as a record fish, I remember turning to Guy and telling him how important it always is to rapidly regain line in a situation like this.

"Now, turn off the motor," I instructed. "Jam the pushpole into the bottom and hold on to it."

From this position, I gradually worked the tarpon away from the island and onto the flat. Halfway to the boat, it careened out in another head-shaker. "At least a hundred thirty pounds," I mumbled out loud.

Now the fish began to behave in a very strange, erratic manner. I thought possibly that a shark might be chasing it, but saw no sign of any other fish nearby. The tarpon darted back and forth in figure eights several times, as if trying to catch its tail. I thought I felt the leader rub across the fin, and it was a sickening thought. Next it made another short run and at the end of it, a magnificent gill-rattling leap. That put more butterflies in my stomach.

But that last run and wild leap seemed to have drained the fight from the fish. Slowly I pumped it in toward the boat and told Guy to grab the gaff and try to hook the fish from right beneath the middle of its belly. You may remember that my rusted lip gaff had broken earlier that day. Now all I had on board was a short-handled hand gaff, and Guy stood ready to use it.

As soon as I worked the tarpon close enough, he made his move and connected. As I knew it would, the tarpon exploded.

> ### "Then it slowly sank in that I had a new fly rod tarpon world record, by 2½ pounds."

Struggling with immense power, the tarpon rapped Guy across the head with the gaff handle. Then it tossed the gaff free into the water about 20 feet away. That should have ended the fight right there.

My chance of ever boating the fish would have been small, almost nonexistent; except that the tide carried the boat directly over the gaff lying in very shallow water.

With one free hand, I reached over the side and retrieved the gaff.

A moment later. I sank it into the tarpon and just held on; there was nothing else to do. When the fish finally stopped plummeting me and the gunwale of the boat, Guy helped me wrestle it aboard.

Then I sat down, wet and weak from the excitement.

Only 18 minutes had elapsed since the fish was hooked. But what an action-packed 18 minutes it had been.

All at once, there in the boat, the fish looked bigger than it had ever appeared in the water. "Probably will go a hundred forty," I said hopefully, "and maybe as much as one-fifty." But to tell the truth, it didn't look as big to me as some other tarpon I've had aboard *Mom's Worry*.

Instead of taking it in to be weighed immediately, I suggested that we go looking for a bigger one.

"Things are working our way," I said to Guy, "so let's not waste time."

During the rest of the afternoon, with me on the pushpole, Guy hooked three more tarpon and landed one, an 80-pounder. We released it.

It wasn't until four hours later that we pulled into the Sea Center dock at Big Pine Key. We hoisted the fish onto the scale operated by Herb Pontin, who is an official weigh-master for the Metropolitan Miami Fishing Tournament.

For a minute, I couldn't believe my eyes when the scales read 151 pounds even.

All at once, I was being pounded on the back and congratulated. Then it slowly sank in that I had a new fly rod tarpon world record, by 2½ pounds. I had caught the largest game fish of any kind ever taken on a fly rod with 12-pound-test leader. How do you describe a moment like that? I can't.

A witnessed affidavit of the catch, a photo, plus my leader and the fly, had to be submitted to Saltwater Fly-Rodders of America for official recognition, which is normally withheld for six months. The record-catching fly, incidentally, had been tied for me by Larry Kreh, the 14-year-old son of fishing and fly casting expert Lefty Kreh from Miami.

But I am not resting on any laurels. Perhaps even while you are reading this story, I will be drifting the Florida flats, fly rod ready to cast. As I said before, there are some 200-pounders waiting to be caught. And I want to be the first fly rodder to catch one.

A young Stu Apte is all smiles as he shows off a nice bonefish caught on a fly.

chapter 5

Bonefish: Hang On and Hope

Writer Zane Grey called bonefish "the gray ghost of the flats." But that's no ghost making the drag on your reel smoke, your heart rate soar, and scaring you with the possibility of taking all your line.

Author Zane Grey gave them a nickname: "the gray ghost of the flats." Probably because one minute you are able to see the silvery bullet of a bonefish under the glare of the foot-deep water, and the next minute it's gone.

Of course, this is part of the mystique that for many anglers makes the bonefish the worthiest of all light-tackle and fly rod opponents. The bonefish is revered and respected with almost fanatic awe, inspiring such comparisons as, "warier than a brown trout," or "quicker than a wahoo," which means "faster than a speeding bullet."

The wily bonefish is all of these. Even though it does not jump, its first electrifying run is the equivalent of having your leader snatched up by a fire-breathing, supercharged, main-event dragster. In a breathless couple of seconds, the hooked bonefish can peel 150 yards off your reel, leaving a frothing V-wake in the shallow water. The only thing you can do is hold on and hope your smoking disk drag is working smoothly enough to let the fish continue its first run until it gets tired enough to stop of its own accord.

To fish for them, you don't have to travel way offshore, or even collect a fancy assortment of heavy boat gear. Bonefish conveniently oblige us by coming right up to the shallow shorelines. Sliding in from deep water, they slip into the shallow flats, sometimes in water from only six inches to a couple of feet deep, hunting for their favorite meal of small crustaceans. With good spinning, plug, or fly tackle, you can hook up with this flashy fighter, which averages around 4 to 6 pounds—big enough to test the most competent angler using 6- to 10-pound-test line.

You are able to fish for them using any number of shallow draft skiffs, but for the greatest thrill, you need to get out of the boat and wade, stalking them on foot.

In 1948, I started fishing one of the best flats in South Florida, to wade for bonefish in Biscayne Bay. It was just south of Cape Florida near a small island called Soldier Key. Actually, Boston Red Sox Baseball Hall of Famer Ted Williams took me there my first time. Over the next few years, I continued exploring the areas farther south. Sands Key, Elliott Key, and Old Rhodes Key. All these areas turned out to be prime bonefish water. One of the very best stretches was a mile-long sand flat just outside Elliott Key.

Yes, you do need a boat to get there, since there are no bridges or ferries to that part of the Key Biscayne National Park, but the trip is well worthwhile. You can launch your boat at Homestead Bayfront Park, planning to arrive during the last hour of the outgoing tide. It is imperative to have a boat that you can pole; otherwise, you will spook the bonefish with the sound of an outboard motor. Pole your boat into the shallowest part of the shoreline it can reach; then drop your anchor. The water will begin rising with the incoming tide, and by the time you get back from wading, the boat will be riding high and easy.

Two fortunate, wading anglers are ready to cast their flies
into a school of feeding bonefish. *Photo by Pat Ford.*

Sometimes the bonefish will come in singles or pairs, but often, they show up in considerable schools, even as many as 20 at a time. It is a sight to watch them come in to feed, often with numerous tails protruding out of the water. If you are lucky enough to have this low tide condition in either the early morning or late afternoon, you can expect the largest numbers of fish. But be aware, they will probably be spookier, too.

The shallower the water, the spookier the bonefish are likely to be. That puts an even more exciting anticipation into the stalk. The challenge is right there in front of you: get too close to the fish, they're gone; cast your fly or bait too close, they're gone; cast too far away, and they don't pick it up. *Arrrgh!*

Bonefish know they're vulnerable in really shallow water. They will spook and flash away at the slightest provocation. I've watched them scare themselves. Muscling up high on a flat to catch a crustacean before the prey can escape, they'll make a splash with their tails and scare themselves right out of a meal. When one fish panics, its commotion may send the whole school, a dozen or more fish, rocketing into headlong flight.

The wariness of the bonefish is nothing if not like the most skittish brown trout, and that vigilance is part of the thrill of the stalk and cast. A small bonefish fly, properly presented, will hit the water softer than a live shrimp. If you're using a spinning rod and casting a live shrimp, the best technique is to cast just beyond the fish and in front of it, then retrieve it so the bait skitters across the surface as though trying to escape.

> ## *"... hiring a bonefish guide*
> ## *was like hiring a pair of eyes."*

The motion and speed of the bait or fly on the retrieve can vary with conditions—from a fast *strip, strip, strip* type of action to a slower, teasing pull. Good guides will help you with the retrieve as they watch your fly and the fish from their lofty perch on a poling platform.

Speaking of guides, I remember that someone once wrote that hiring a bonefish guide was like hiring a pair of eyes. True enough, because bonefish can be hard to see. Even with good glasses picking out their shapes and movements, it takes time and practice to master the skill. Add in a lot of overhead clouds and choppy windy conditions, and the difficulties reach the frustration stage. Guides and experienced anglers sometimes make the most of unfavorable conditions by seeking "muds," created by a pod of feeding fish, or anchoring beside a piece of white sandy bottom where the fish can be seen as they come to chum.

A bonefish is, as they say about gold, where you find it. It can be a lot of other places, too, and thereby hangs the tale of your fishing day. Where are they? What are they doing?

You might be lucky enough to check into a condominium in the Bahamas and at the crack of dawn, or at sunset, when there is virtually no breeze, find bonefish tailing on a flat right near your lodging. Or perhaps you are experienced and resourceful enough to find bonefish while scouting the waters on your own, checking out flats you can reach at roadsides. Have at it!

Capt. Rick Murphy, one of the all-time great captains in South Florida, wants to get this hefty fly-rod bonefish back into the water as soon as possible. *Photo by Pat Ford.*

Bones go to different flats during different tides, at various times of the year, and for different reasons. What all that means for most anglers is that guides are necessary. You need a guide who has fished those flats day in and day out year-round.

During all the years I was such a guide in one of the Florida Keys, I like to think I showed my clients the best of bonefishing. The biggest bonefish I ever saw, however, did not come along when I was poling a client. Here's how it happened:

One afternoon after completely wearing out a husband-and-wife client out fighting big tarpon, I was home early enough to take Bernice, my wife of one year, out to hopefully catch her first bonefish. It was less than a ten-minute run to Coupon Bight, an area that I thought would have a perfect bonefish tide.

I eased up from the deeper water to a strip bank, picked up my pushpole, and started to slowly pole down the bank. Less than ten minutes after we arrived there, a small school of about six nice bonefish came cruising by, close enough for an easy cast. But Bernice had problems getting the shrimp to the fish with her new spinning rod. Either she could not see them on the edge of the deeper water, or her cast would go awry.

It was now getting a little late in the day. Far down in the West, the sun was creating a glare, making it difficult to see through the surface of the water in the distance.

Up closer, we did see a few bonnethead sharks, and I was trying to explain the difference of how a bonefish looks and a shark looks in the water in order to be able to identify each one.

Looking quite a ways down the bank, I could see a fish going along slowly, probably looking for a goodie. I pointed it out to her, saying, "Do you see that one way down there? You can tell that is a shark because it's too big to be a bonefish and because of its brownish color." I also told her to just keep watching it, because as it got closer, she would be able to see what I meant.

We both stood there without even a spinning rod in our hands, watching this large fish coming closer, and closer. Suddenly it decided things didn't look right and turned to head for the deeper water.

The vision slammed home! It was a bonefish of at least 20 pounds! By far the biggest I had ever seen anywhere.

There I was, rigged with a spinning rod, 8-pound line, and a perfect live shrimp. Before I could reach down, the fish vanished into the depths, taking with it my chance to catch the ultimate bonefish world record.

There have been only a few times in my guiding and overall fishing career that I misjudged a fish. That was the one that truly cost me. Since that was one of my favorite areas to fish, I poled along that bank many times after that day, eyes always peeled for Mr. Big. I never saw him again.

During two of the best days I experienced as a bonefish guide, back in the early 1960s, my clients, a man and wife, hooked 29 bonefish and landed 19; the smallest was about 6½ pounds, the largest probably 10 pounds. After fighting bonefish all day, they were too tired to go out early the next day, though they had booked me in advance. Finally, they did go out around 10 A.M., and again had a fabulous day, with 23 bonefish on, and 17 landed. It does take some arm muscle to fight bonefish, even small ones; they can quickly convince you they have more than you bargained for in strength and tenacity by fighting for 10 to 30 minutes, depending on the angler.

Unfortunately, those glory days of bonefishing in the Islamorada–Key Largo area are not happening anymore. The fisheries biologists with Bonefish Tarpon Trust (BTT) are diligently working to find out what has happened to the bonefish fishery we had 20 or 30 years ago. If and when you have the opportunity to join that magnificent organization, please do!

A couple of times each year, my wife and I go to the Bahamas for bonefishing as it used to be in the Florida Keys. During the past 30 years, I have fished 75 percent of the island fisheries in the Bahamas. One of the places I like best is the fairly new, Black Fly Lodge on Abaco Island. Depending on the wind conditions, time of year, and so forth, their guides trail a skiff sometimes 20 or 30 miles to put you into a protected area for bonefishing.

My last time there was when Black Fly Lodge had a grand opening of its Legends suites. They have a plaque on each room with the names of those anglers they considered truly great. They have the Lefty Kreh suite, Flip Pallot room, Joan Wulff suite, Chico Fernandez suite, Pat Ford suite, José Wejebe (*Spanish Fly*) suite, and the Stu Apte suite. And we each got to stay in our "own room."

We were all there except for José, who had lost his life in a plane crash nine months before that gathering.

Because they had one room (José's) available, the lodge did an Internet auction for the highest bidder to spend three nights and four days fishing, drinking, dining, and getting to know each of us. The money was a donation to Bonefish Tarpon Trust (BTT). I fished with the winning gentleman for one day, and we have since become good friends. That day, we landed 24 bonefish on flies between us, including a couple of doubleheaders.

I'm 84 years old, and unfortunately, I can no longer get out of the boat to wade, because of my balance. But the area we were fishing had a beautiful, level, white sand bottom. So my fishing partner of the day got out to wade. Some of the doubleheaders we caught were with him in the water and me in the boat, steadying myself with a leaning bar on the bow.

And I could see Joan Wulff, about 200 or 300 yards away, fighting bonefish while she was wading. The next day, a cold front moved in over our wonderful Bahamian retreat and we had overcast skies with 20- to 30-mile-an-hour winds blowing horizontal rain throughout the day. Those of us who went fishing in the rain still caught many bonefish on flies. There were massive schools of big bonefish gathering in 2 to 3 feet of water to go out into the deep water to spawn.

Fortunately, Aaron Adams, PhD (and Director of Operations for BTT), was there with a fairly large crew, taking samples and tagging some of the bonefish with sonic tags, doing research on where and when these bonefish spawn.

As far as the future of the bonefish in the Florida Keys, I am sure that just like the striped bass of the Northeastern United States, which fell on hard times for a few years, bonefish will someday be back in the Keys in numbers bonefish addicts will appreciate.

A silver dollar-sized crab bait, fished with spinning tackle, lured this monster permit to Capt. Sean O'Keefe's boat during a Redbone Slam Tournament in Key West, Florida.

chapter 6

In Praise of Permit

Years ago, not many people knew they existed. Today, the pursuit
of permit has become an angling craze. I'll try to show you what
the excitement is all about and why you should join the fun.

It was a cool spring day some years ago as we headed offshore from old Key West. We had spent half the night catching finny crabs in a dip net at Shark Key Viaduct Bridge near Key West.

I was with my good friend and new fishing guide José Wejebe in his boat the *Spanish Fly*. Back then, José was a young man who had learned a lot about fishing in his few short years. He was a talented amateur and promising pro. We launched at Garrison Bight and ran a 20-minute leg to a group of shallow flats in the direction of the Marquesas Keys. José wanted to find a fish to beat my current 38-pound International Game Fish Association record on 6-pound line, which has stood for a number of years.

Permit can be a formidable foe on the flats. A deep-body fish, member of the pompano family, it makes a first run that puts the bonefish to shame in speed and power. And, being much larger, permit require a lot more finesse when they get a big belly of 6-pound line stringing out behind them.

We arranged our run to arrive at the beginning of the incoming tide. It is the very best time to take permit, which don't like to be caught high up on the shallows on an outgoing tide. They like a quick getaway to deep water when spooked, and they can be extremely skittish.

Stu brought this world record permit to the hands of his companion
Bob Whitaker in 21 minutes. At 47 pounds, the permit was an
International Spin Fishing Association record.

We found lots of fish, but they were not being too receptive to my offerings. Their big forked tails were everywhere on the wide flats, poking out of the water like black sickles as the fish bent to feed on crustaceans. These weren't big fish, at least not in the record range we wanted. They'd average about 20 pounds.

The wind was calm, and each time I cast the crab, I'd get too close and spook them, or too far away and not get any interest. The silver-dollar-size crab is hooked through the point-edge of its shell so it can swim freely. Then it is cast about 4 feet from the

target, with the line being stopped at the last moment as you gently raise your rod tip so the bait drops in naturally and skitters across the surface, making it look like an escaping crab, just the meal ticket to a permit.

I cast about 20 times without a take. Some fish would ignore me and keep on dipping down five or six times right beside my bait. Then I saw a pair of fish, apart from the rest, feeding together. I've been known to tell anglers that the best cast you can make is the one they take, and though this cast was a little too splashy, the permit charged. It ran up on the bait, gulping it down in one bite.

When it turned to swim off, I banged it— three or four short, sharp strokes to set the hook. And the fireworks began. Streaking off in a wake of foam and streamers, ripping line from my little Sigma 0002 plug-casting reel, it headed for deep water in a panic.

The fish was so wild, it ran right to a group of sunning sharks—big 350-pounders—and spooked them, too. They started scattering, and I was sure one of them would brush my light 6-pound-class line and ping it off. But none did.

The permit ran on, heading for deep water and safety, while we fired up the engine to follow it. There was no way I could turn a 25-pound permit in full flight with 6-pound-class monofilament line. We stayed about 30 yards behind the fleeing fish, and I kept the pressure on until finally it ran out of steam.

Then I was able to honk back on the rig. Within 15 minutes, the fish lay panting at the gunwale, and I asked José to tail it for me. That was something he had never done before, but it's easy to accomplish. For the kind of fish permit is, with a narrow, deep body pinched in right at the base of the tail, grabbing hold of it there is the best way. You don't damage the fish, and you get the thrill of feeling that strength and power in your hand. He reached down and tailed the fish, then lifted it right out. I grabbed my very accurate Chatillon scale, which I carried in the boat for just that purpose. The fish weighed 33 pounds—not quite a new record, but still fun on 6-pound-class line.

We shot a few pictures, removed the hook, and gently slipped the permit back into the water. After a few seconds, it swam off just like brand-new. This was the *Spanish Fly*'s first permit.

Note: After I originally wrote this article, José Wejebe and his *Spanish Fly* boat went on to become world-famous icons on fishing TV programs. His shows were watched by millions of dedicated fans. Tragically, his climb to fame ended on April 6, 2004, when the single-engine plane he was piloting in a takeoff from Everglades City, Florida, suddenly dived into the ground because of a probable wind shear created by a fast-moving cold front. The plane was an "experimental amateur-built" type, not generally well regarded for safety. Fifty-four years old, José was an experienced pilot with 1,000 hours. Obviously, something went very, very wrong with that takeoff. José is deeply missed by all who knew him and fished with him, and by his legions of loyal fans.

To a great many saltwater fly anglers, catching a large permit on a fly is the Holy Grail of fly fishing, and maybe it should be. Back in the late 1950s and early 1960s, you could count the number of permit caught on a fly with the fingers on one hand. But as a result of the numerous fly innovations and amount of upgraded angler abilities, catching a permit on a fly, especially in places like Belize, Mexico's Yucatán, and some of the flats in Cuba, has almost become commonplace. Maybe not quite so commonplace, many permit are caught fly fishing on the flats throughout the Florida Keys as well.

Actually, I have caught more permit on tarpon flies than I have on permit flies. Normally, I like fishing permit with either a spinning rod or a bait-casting rod using a silver-dollar-size live blue crab, as I explained before. The ones I have caught on tarpon flies were when I have been tarpon fishing on rough windy days and I would see a permit, generally a big one, and cast my tarpon fly rigged with 12 inches of 80-pound bite tippet. Probably one out of every three I cast to would charge and eat the fly.

One windy rough day on the ocean, I cast to and hooked a permit I know had to weigh more than 50 pounds. I was using a 12-pound-test tippet with 12 inches of 80-pound bite tippet. With that kind of a leader setup, I knew there was no way this monster permit could get away. It screamed line off my reel, faster than a locomotive, quickly getting into my backing. Then, I thought it was running back at me as my line went slack. I was winding line like a demon and almost wound the fly into the fly rod's tip-top. My tarpon fly was tied on an Eagle Claw #254 SS, 4/0 hook that I had sharpened for great tarpon penetration. The hook was bent into a circle. Evidently, when this permit engulfed my fly, it had it in its crushers and did a number on the hook.

Permit, like bonefish, have shell crushers in their jaws; I've heard they can apply as much as 3,000 pounds of pressure per square inch, which they use for crushing shellfish and small conch. One day, fishing in a Florida Keys area called Content Pass with my dear friend and mentor, Joe Brooks, it looked like we had hit the permit mother lode. The tide was just deep enough for what seemed like hundreds of permit to come into the area, and we could see tails everywhere.

I personally watched a number of those big permit dip down with their coal-black tails penetrating the surface of the water and pick up a shell, chomp down on it, then eject the small shell fragments. Later, using my bait net, I scooped up some of those little white spiraled shellfish. That evening I put them on a concrete slab and tried to break them open with a hammer. You can't believe how tough it was. I eventually broke some, but it wasn't easy.

As it seems to so often happen with permit, the biggest one I ever hooked and caught came as a sudden target of opportunity. I was actually fishing for tarpon, without even having the correct bait or my tackle rigged for permit. It was a beautiful sunny afternoon with a very light breeze and an incoming tide on an ocean-side, white sand flat near Bahia Honda Rail Bridge.

I selected this spot because I had promised to help an old friend catch his first tarpon on a fly. Bob Whitaker was the outdoor editor of the *Arizona Republic* newspaper. I knew Bob had never even cast a fly to a tarpon in his life, so I picked that spot knowing he would be able to really see the schools of tarpon that I was reasonably sure would be floating by on the incoming tide.

During the next three hours of the tide, Bob probably made 30 casts to big tarpon, hooking at least ten of them, breaking some of them off while others would do the tarpon thing, throwing the fly on one of their wild jumps.

All the while I was giving Bob instructions on what to do and how to go about doing it, he was seeing hundred-pound-type tarpon in 4½ feet of gin-clear water. A spectacle like that has a tendency to bring out all kinds of buck fever. Bob finally asked me to take the fly rod and cast to the next bunch of tarpon that came by in order to show him exactly how to do what I had been telling him.

The first fish I cast to was probably an honest 110 pounds, and I managed to bring it to the boat in less than 20 minutes, without even pulling up our anchor and possibly losing our perfect spot to another boat.

"Okay, Stu," Bob said. "I think I know what you have been telling me, but I don't know if I can do it the way you do."

About that time, a big permit came swimming by our anchored boat. That prompted me to holler to Cal Cochran, another guide in the second spot, asking him if he had any permit crabs. He quickly replied to come on over, and I told him I'd be there in a minute.

First, I wanted to tie a hook onto my ultralight spinning outfit. Without even doing a Bimini twist to create a double line, I tied a 2/0 hook directly to the 6-pound-test line. I quickly unhooked from my anchor line, leaving the anchor and buoy there, then poled over to Cal's boat and got a single crab. I hooked it through one wing, dropped it in the water, and poled back to my anchor line.

Almost like clockwork, after I hooked the boat back to the anchor line, Bob had another shot at a group of tarpon and got one to eat. He set the hook, but it quickly jumped off. While he was stripping his fly line in to check his leader, I happened to look in the area where I had spotted that first big permit.

There was what looked to be a twin of the first fish. I picked up my ultralight spinning rod with a Penn 722 ultralight spinning reel and 6-pound-test monofilament line. I quickly opened the bail and flipped the crab slightly in front and slightly on the other side of where this big permit was moving. In order to soften the presentation of the crab hitting the water, I put my first finger down, feathering the cast. When the crab hit the water, I slightly raised my rod, making the bait skid across the top of the water the way a frightened crab might do.

You would think that permit hadn't eaten for weeks, the way it charged the crab, engulfing it. When I set the hook, it took off for parts unknown, out in the ocean, heading for Hawk Channel and deep water. By the time I managed to get my outboard engine started and do a quick disconnect from my anchor line, this big permit had more than two-thirds of my 6-pound-test monofilament off the reel.

Bob did know how to run a boat, and he did a excellent job getting me toward this wild permit while I wound line back on the reel.

I asked Bob if he had ever gaffed any fish in his life of basically freshwater bass fishing, and he said absolutely and unequivocally that he had not. Not wanting to take a chance of having him tail this big critter, I had him use a little tarpon release hand gaff, and he did an excellent job. I wasn't sure if this was the largest permit ever taken on rod and reel, but I knew it would be close.

Some hours later when we got it to a tackle shop in Marathon, Florida, that had an official world record scale, it ended up weighing an even 47 pounds. At that time, it was the second-largest permit ever caught on a rod and reel. Back then, IGFA (International Game Fish Association) had not started keeping line class records under 12-pound class, so it went into the 12-pound-class record book. I also entered it into the ISFA (International Spin Fishing Association) for records on spinning equipment.

Facing. Stu was using a Penn 722 reel with an ultralight Ted Williams spinning rod.

I have a Pflueger skin mount of that big permit on my wall with the 8-by-10-inch framed certificate of record under it, along with a picture of Bob Whitaker holding the fish out of the water by its tail.

Now for the funny ending to this happening. That evening, Capt. Cal Cochran called me and said that his angler said Stu Apte has to be the luckiest fisherman in the whole world. First he catches a big tarpon on fly without even chasing it down, and does it in less than 20 minutes. Then he catches a monster permit on light line and does that in a timed 21 minutes.

Cal broke up laughing two or three times while he was telling me about his angler, who caught a 18½-pound permit last year on 25-pound-test spin, landing it in an hour and 48 minutes.

"He also fought an eighty-pound tarpon," Cal said, "using a twenty-pound-test tippet, for two and a half hours before losing it. And this guy believes the only reason you can catch these fish as quickly as you always do is because you are so lucky to hook the easy ones."

I'll take all the luck I can get. But the truth is, when catching big fish like permit and tarpon on light tackle, it has a lot to do with how you fight the fish. This comes with experience and some special techniques.

But, that's another story.

chapter 7

Pacific Sailfish on a Fly: The Start of Something Big

How battling Pacific sailfish with a fly rod started at jungle lodge 100 miles from the nearest lightbulb!

How would you like to cast your fly to a fish that's longer than your fly rod?

That's right—longer than your 9-foot fly rod. If you want an adrenaline rush almost equal to landing a jet on an aircraft carrier, try a Pacific sailfish on a fly! You will be close up and personal with your adversary, and it's not so difficult to make happen as you might believe.

In more than 40 years of fly fishing for Pacific sail, I've helped scores of people catch their first. My first was at Club de Pesca Panama (now called Tropic Star Lodge) in 1964.

Picture this scenario: The ocean, glassy smooth, as the Pacific often is. The sky, gray and almost threatening, a thunderstorm brewing on the horizon. Your crew has rigged three soft-head teasers with the belly-strip from a bonito sewn inside. Suddenly the tip of a bill appears behind the far teaser. You feel this in your gut; a sailfish is checking out your teaser.

Your captain or mate sees it first and shouts, "He's coming, he's coming!" Or, *"Vela! Vela!"* That's "Sail! Sail!"

Your David–Goliath adventure is about to begin. In about three seconds, all hell is going to break loose. The sail will grab the teaser, but the mate will snatch it away. Two or three times. Now the sail is mad as hell. That's when you drop that popper 3 feet behind its tail.

After inhaling an Enrico Puglisi billfish fly, this Pacific sailfish launches
the kind of high-jumping antics that makes it a fly-fishing favorite.

Now your tackle and fish-playing abilities are about to be stretched to the redline maximum.

This kind of action is fairly common today, but actually started in October 1964, when oil tycoon Ray Smith called me from his office in Dallas, Texas, to ask if I would meet him for dinner that night at the Miami International Airport's hotel restaurant. He said he was catching the early flight to Panama the morning after our meeting. He indicated he wanted to discuss something I would probably find very interesting.

Did I ever! Over dinner, he told me about the camp he'd carved out of the Panamanian jungle, in a location that was over 100 miles from the nearest electric lightbulb.

I felt ready, willing, and able to check out this far-flung fishing paradise. The thought of fishing a newly discovered, remote hot spot had me ready to pack my things. At that stage of my life, anything pertaining to fishing was of great interest, and my December 1964 trip to Club de Pesca Panama was to be the beginning of a completely new fishing world to me.

On my first trip, we flew from Panama City in a twin-engine C-45 Beechcraft, along with two other passengers, a crate with two pigs, and one large container of chickens. We landed at a World War II U.S. Army Air Corps emergency landing strip, near the little village of Hockey. After a half-mile walk to the river, we walked a gangplank to board a 31-foot Bertram. Next we ran a treacherous sandbar with large cresting waves at the mouth of the river to make our 20-minute run to Club de Pesca. There we climbed out of the Bertram onto a large dugout canoe for a 100-yard slow ride to the beach, where we rolled up our pants legs and waded ashore on the dark volcanic sand.

On a typical fishing day, when we began exploring those waters, the action began when our mate, Lucho, saw a sailfish jump at least a quarter mile off our starboard beam. Immediately Capt. Jamie Archibald turned the 31-foot Bertram sharply, increasing his rpm at the same time in order to lead the direction of the fish and make an intercept. As we approached the area where the fish had leaped, Archie reduced the throttle setting to a fast trolling speed. The mate put a pair of artificial squid teasers over the side.

Suddenly bills appeared behind each teaser. The mate slowly reeled the squid teasers just out of reach of the fish, moving them just fast enough to keep them away from the slashing bills of the excited sailfish. I slipped a belly bait with a hook into the water. The fish lunged at my bait, and the ferocious battle began. When it ended, I had landed another record fish.

The next ten days were nothing but fishing and relaxing. I was in the middle of doing them both real well when Ray popped the question. He made me a very interesting offer: "Would you consider leaving Pan Am to become the general manager of Club de Pesca Panama?"

Manager? Me? After being in this gorgeous setting for ten days, after sampling the lifestyle and the fishing, I was quite tempted. But I had to admit to him that I had already heard through the grapevine that managers didn't last long around there.

I tactfully explained to Ray that the only way I would quit Pan Am to take such a position was a ten-year guaranteed salary. At that time, because the fishing was so seasonal and would not require my presence at the camp for the entire year, we negotiated $25,000 a year. But Ray inevitably balked at meeting my ten-year guarantee, so the deal to be his manager fizzled.

We did negotiate a deal, however, that was more to my liking. I agreed to take a 90-day leave of absence from Pan Am the next year, 1965, and go down to the club to teach his captains and mates about light-tackle fishing, fly fishing, catch-and-release conservation methods and take some of his guests out on charters. He was thrilled by my offer and showed it by more than doubling my Pan Am salary.

Dr. Neil Rogers demonstrates the proper way to bow to a leaping sailfish.

When I returned in May 1965 for a three-month stay, the camp had an amphibian Goose airplane, and we landed on the water, taxied up to the beach, lowered the landing gear, and rolled right up on the shore without getting our feet wet. A great start for a three-month adventure.

There were many great happenings during those three months. I caught a 58-pound dolphin (dorado, mahimahi) fly fishing with 12-pound-class tippet, which is still the longest-standing saltwater fly rod world record. And I caught the first Pacific sailfish ever caught fly fishing. That, too, was with 12-pound-class tippet.

The sailfishing was something to dream about. I caught two more world record Pacific sailfish, including a 128-pounder that I beat a month later with a 136-pounder, which is the second-longest still-standing saltwater fly rod world record on 12-pound-class tippet. And there were other records, like the 28-pound yellowfin tuna and a 24-pound jack crevalle fly rod records, to mention a couple.

World-renowned angler, author, and filmmaker Lee Wulff came down for a week of fishing and filming, and I helped him catch his first sailfish ever on a fly rod. There was a great film crew from Hollywood, California, filming the fishing half of a pilot film for a new network television series, *The Big Ones.* They had already filmed the hunting half with Fred Bear bow-hunting polar bear in northern Alaska. They happened to be on the scene in a second boat when I was fighting and landed my 136-pound record sailfish. They also had some great footage of Scottie Yeager, a lovely lady from Palm Beach, Florida, one of the founders of the International Women's Fishing Association (IWFA).

In the early years of fishing the bountiful Piñas Bay, there would be many other film crews on hand and magazine writers who spread the fame of big water, big fish, on light tackle. I produced an *American Sportsman* show there that won a prestigious Teddy award.

Catching sailfish with a fly rod has spread to many popular destinations today— to the delight of a great number of anglers. But it all started there at Club de Pesca Panama, now Tropic Star Lodge, a remote tropical paradise and a fishery to dream about.

Stu's 200th Pacific sailfish on a fly gets a lingering look before it goes back into the water.

Watching a Pacific sailfish leap is like watching a Polaris missile.

With a gator bass on his line, Capt. Ralph Delph sets the hook as hard as he can.

chapter 8

Gator Bass

We call these Everglades bigmouths "gator bass."
They're mean, hungry, and big.

In many parts of the country, anglers put away their gear as soon as the weather begins to deteriorate in the fall, and don't pick it up again until springtime.

Even in Florida where I live, it's true that winter seas offshore can be upsetting, and colder water inshore can often discourage flats fishing. Of course, some of us die-hards continue to fish no matter what. And we'll catch a lot of fish, too. Mackerel, bluefish, and kingfish move in—and, yes, sailfish show up in abundance to feed on the shallow reefs. Some of the freshwater fishing begins to peak in the cool autumn weather. Barring a storm or maverick cold front, you can fish in relative comfort.

I used to spend an occasional fall day with friends bass fishing when I did not want to get beat up in the crashing seas from a passing northerner. I used my backcountry skiff that worked so well for me on the flats, and much of the light saltwater tackle I use spinning or casting is perfectly applicable to bass fishing. So no extra gear is necessary.

I like to fish from a skiff in the shallow water, poling it along the same way I do on the flats. On one trip 30 years ago, fishing with Flip Pallot and Ralph Delph in 3- to 4-foot-deep waters in the Everglades, I found the vegetation was so thick, you could hardly spot the fish. Casting required the same kind of pinpoint accuracy you need for bonefish and permit.

Above. Flip Pallot, on the left, and Ralph Delph are reliving some of the day's gator bass action.

Facing top. A Johnson weedless spoon and a chartreuse plastic worm brought gator bass crashing through the lily pads.

Facing bottom. A bass-eye view of the Johnson weedless spoon and chartreuse plastic worm.

The saw grass, pepper grass, and lily pads would swish softly as they parted, letting the boat pass through, and then close again, hardly leaving any sign we had been there. When the prize is a lunker bass that may go more than 10 pounds, a serious angler instinctively crouches down like the predator he is, and we three were no exceptions.

While I poled the boat, Ralph stood in the bow, watching for the V-wake pushed up by a big cruising fish. We were stalking "gator bass," the nickname we used for the monstrous bass lurking there. Suddenly, Ralph held up his hand. I halted the boat.

"Big bass, a gator bass, pushing water," he whispered. He eased himself over the side, and the chest-high water swirled around his waders.

Ralph moved into close position and executed a perfect cast a few feet ahead of a moving wake in a patch of thick, green water hyacinth. The weedless spoon-worm lure plopped down and was retrieved just fast enough to keep the combination on the surface. Tension mounted as the lure and the wake quickly converged upon each other. Then, in a flash, the water opened up and a monstrous head appeared, mouth gasping, to snatch the lure.

"Got 'im!" Ralph yelled. The fight was short, decisive, and final. He brought the big fish wallowing up to the boat as if it were a wild-eyed tarpon, beaten but still defiant. I marveled at the similarities between this kind of fishing and stalking any number of fish on the flats when everything goes right—a slow, poling stalk; sighting the target; and then one cast, one hell of a quick fight, one fish. With the almost-unparalleled excitement of flats fishing.

For this close-cover "in-fighting," I like bait-casting tackle, but tough spinning or spin-cast will also work in the heavy brush. The important thing is to use a rod with medium to stiff action. That lets you manhandle the fish through the weeds and grass before it can get too deep and tangled. It's important to keep a tight line and hold the fish high. If it gets too far down, into the "veggies," it's good-bye, bass.

A 12- or 15-pound-test line worked well on my casting reel, the same as I used for snook or tarpon in the Keys. With spinning gear, I would sometimes go as light as 8 pounds, but because of the pepper grass and hyacinth, I'd often use 10-pound-test monofilament. (That was then, but now I would be using 20-pound-test braid on the casting outfit and 12-pound-test braid on the spinning, giving me a decisive advantage.)

Probably the most important part of the gear for these backcountry lunkers is the lure. A number 1230 Johnson Silver or Gold Minnow is my favorite choice. At times, the slightly larger spoon, number 1310, also works well when the fish are running big.

I add a 6- to 9-inch chartreuse plastic worm to the weedless hook for a couple of reasons. First, the worm seems to be irresistible to a hungry or angry bass; second, it keeps the tail end of the spoon down, so it's truly weedless. Rigged that way, it

can flutter right across the weeds, no matter how thick, and seemingly climb up and over the pepper grass. I still use similar rigs fishing for snook and redfish in the backcountry of the Keys.

Having caught the first fish, Ralph was unanimously elected by Flip and me to tow the boat along while we searched the tight cover for more. The grass was not so high, and while we could see the fish better from the boat, we figured the fish would also be able to see us. We dismounted into the cool chest-deep water. Traveling light, I tucked an extra spoon into the chest pocket of my waders along with a handful of 7-inch-long chartreuse plastic worms.

Casting across a little patch of clear water, I dropped my lure in the grass on the other side. I worked it back over the green carpet. Just as it hit the clear pool, a big bass boiled up and smashed it. Playing it tough, I managed to horse the fish away from the weeds for three beautiful jumps, but then it dived and stopped all the action in an ugly tangle of pepper grass. I quickly waded over to the spot and reached down to get the fish loose. It was a nice 7-pounder. I released it to grow up into a leviathan; there were more fighters waiting.

The best two fish of the day were a 9-pounder Flip brought in and a 10-plus-pounder by Ralph. If we had kept everything we landed, the average would have gone close to 4 pounds. I'd say that in the saw grass of South Florida, four out of ten fish caught will weigh more than 5 pounds. I know there are some 15-pounders out there; we've had them on. But the heavy ones are also the smart ones. They dig down in the grass and pull free.

By the time we had all circled back to the boat and hoisted anchor for the run back, we had released 25 bass, and Flip and Ralph kept just a few for the freezer. They thought the bass you find way out back in the Glades, where the water is clear and clean, are about the best-tasting freshwater fish you could ask for.

They may not be tarpon, snook, or redfish, but when the weather keeps us off the flats, these saw grass bass offer a special escape for anglers who won't be kept home.

Facing. A younger, beardless Flip Pallot looking into a gator bass gullet filled with a Johnson spoon and plastic worm.

Guide Jim Louden joins Stu in admiring a
New Zealand brown trout. *Photo by Bernice Apte.*

chapter 9

The Best Trout Streams I've Ever Fished

You're going to want to buy a ticket to New Zealand.

I'm about to make a couple of bold statements, but I can do it with the knowledge of a pilot committed to landing his fighter jet on the pitching deck of an aircraft carrier. No hesitation. No backing off. No "ifs" and "maybes."

New Zealand brown trout fishing is the finest on earth. And the Mataura River on the southern end of South Island is the finest dry fly trout stream in the world.

While the journey from Miami to South Island, New Zealand, takes one to the far side of the globe and into the opposite of whatever season we're in, what's that to a Pan Am pilot who happens to be an avid angler? Why, nothing at all.

The Mataura River practically runs through my friend George Kennedy's backyard. George managed a slaughterhouse a few miles downriver from his property and felt as passionate about trout fishing as I did.

I made my first visit there in 1969, and after dinner, George took us to a spot about three miles behind his house for my first look at these fabled waters. I peeked over a high bank and gazed into the clear, ambling river.

A number of brown trout were gently cruising on the surface, where an eddy in the current created a good place to feed. Some of those fish would have weighed as much as 10 pounds, and it was not easy for me to just stand there and watch them.

But the steep bank was no place from which to fish, and after all, we were just dinner guests. So I made a careful mental note as to the location, and two hours later, af-

59

ter having made my excuses to the Kennedy family, I was chest deep in water, making 90-foot dry fly presentations from the other side of the Mataura to those same trout.

These beauties had not been pressured much, because, for the most part, New Zealanders don't bother to cast that far for their fish. With such an abundance of trout at that time, they didn't have to. But 90-foot casts were the only way to this bunch. At that distance, I was still able to take two. Of course, I missed four or five others because with so much line out there, it created the inevitable big line bow, and setting the hook was tricky. The biggest trout I caught that evening weighed only 6 pounds. Only 6 pounds? I can't really say I was brokenhearted.

The Mataura wanders through rolling countryside in sight of snow-clad peaks, which provide a backdrop of unbelievable grandeur to match the unbelievable fishing. I found the Mataura River itself reminiscent of Henrys Fork of the Snake River in Idaho. Most of the people who live in this part of New Zealand are descendants of the Scots, and at times you get the feeling you are fishing in Scotland. Fishing guide Peter Cullen even referred to our small dry flies as "wee lures."

But most impressive of all to me was the manner in which the Mataura is fished. While I did have to wade in deep to reach those trout behind the Kennedy home, that was the exception rather than the rule. Some mornings I never even bothered to don my waders, because I knew I would be able to fish successfully from the bank all day. These banks were about 4 feet above the level of the river, and I would walk upstream until I saw a trout large enough to deserve a presentation.

Streamside lunches are popular in New Zealand. Here Stu is asking guide Jim Louden if this particular brown trout should be a lunch "keeper." *Photo by Bernice Apte.*

I would quickly crouch to keep out of sight while I kept an eye on exactly where that fish was, casting from a lower profile so as not to spook it. Occasionally, I would have to get into the water, because debris or some other obstruction on the land would prevent a clear presentation. More often, I'd simply cast from the bank. Most of those presentations were within 50 feet, and sometimes I would even get as close as 20.

The main point is that all the fishing I did was selective casting of dry flies to trout I could clearly see. This was my kind of fishing, for it reminded me of stalking bonefish on the flats near my Florida Keys home.

Much of the Mataura River, like the stretch on the Kennedy land, is on private property. While in many areas of the world, that could prevent the average angler from reaching the riverbank, in the area of the Mataura—which is called Southland and is the southernmost province of the country—when I fished there, agreements had been reached with many landowners to keep permanent or semipermanent routes to the river open to the public.

Generally speaking, New Zealand fly fishing is best from the beginning of December (their summer) on, but as I'll relate later, I experienced a hatch during my November trip that was nothing short of spectacular. In fact, during my trip I caught more than 100 brown trout, and only one of those fish weighed less than 2 pounds. The average trout went about 3½ pounds, but I also caught many 5- and 6-pounders. While November may be considered a preseason month by New Zealand standards, I really had no complaints.

The only November problem I encountered was seagull nesting. I found them all along the banks of the Mataura, and they were bothersome when they flew near me because their shadows occasionally spooked the fish.

I can also report that these browns were the hardest fighting I have caught anywhere. The female trout, called hen-fish by the New Zealanders, were the most active and did the most jumping.

While the Mataura River browns run big, the flies they like best run small. Sizes 14, 16, and at times even 18 in any of the quill ties are productive. Early in the season, the 12s and 14s are used, but after the beginning of December, when the water temperature begins to rise and the days begin to lengthen, the smaller hatches are more frequent. This applies particularly to the lower Mataura.

As to patterns, I recommend buying flies locally wherever you are fishing. I was able to purchase the necessary flies in the town of Gore at the tackle shop. They were well tied, and the Mataura trout liked them just fine. I used the following patterns successfully: Peveril, Red Tip Governor, Kahaki (the natives pronounce it with three syllables), Queen, Greenwell's Glory, Quill Cochy-Bondhu, Dad's Favorite, Twilight Beauty, and Green Manuka Beetle.

As an example of the right tackle, I think it's worth mentioning that I was using a three-piece, 5-weight, 8-foot fiberglass rod with a matching reel and line. Sometimes I would use a double-taper or sometimes a weight-forward line. With such an outfit, your cast can reach the fish without too much danger of spooking them. People using heavier line, however, do spook the fish. Of course, a perfect compromise outfit is not always just exactly right for each given situation. What I needed when I was making those early 90-foot presentations was a floating shooting head with monofilament running line. That setup would have enabled me to make the long casts with a minimum of line drag, and I would have lost fewer fish.

However, everything was in working order on what I must rate as one of the finest days of freshwater fishing I have ever experienced. It began about 1 P.M., when I saw fish rising from my car window. I parked near the Otoma Flat Bridge, waded in, and in rather short order I took six brown trout on a size 18 Dad's Favorite dry fly, similar to a Quill Gordon. And, as usual, I had missed a number of others.

After this action subsided somewhat, I walked upstream for about a mile and was just rounding a bend when I saw a large shape swimming upstream in about 4 feet of water.

I knew it was the biggest brown I had ever seen.

I immediately wished that I had a big streamer tied on. But right then was no time to change flies. I had to take a shot with what I had.

I cast the Dad's Favorite about 8 feet in front of the moving target. I simply could not believe my own eyes as I watched that monster brown come up off the bottom. It was huge, and it simply engulfed that tasty little tidbit I had placed in its path. The fight that followed can only be described as rough-and-tumble and I somewhat sheepishly admit to wading right out to the fish and standing directly over it while fighting.

After 15 minutes of this, the big trout finally tired enough for me to work him back into the shallows. It was so shallow, the fish was swimming on its side just to stay in the water. As I gently tried to beach it, the old fellow gave a big flop back toward deeper water, and since I was using only a 2-pound tippet, I naturally let him have his head. However, he was pretty tired, and I was soon able to lead him around again toward the beach. Then, just as I was certain I had him, he shook his head once, and to my utter dismay, I saw my prize break off and swim slowly away. I could easily have kicked it back onto the beach with my foot, but believing he had earned his freedom through a fault of mine, I resisted the urge. Had I lost a 200-pound tarpon on fly, I could not have felt more dejected.

Facing. The New Zealand mountains provide the setting while brown trout provide the action for one of Stu's favorite trout fishing adventures. *Photo by Bernice Apte.*

I soon discovered that it was not the tippet that had broken, but the hook. For some reason, it had snapped high on the shank above the bend. I am pretty good at guesstimating the weight of fish, and this brown trout would have topped 15 pounds for sure, and to my eye looked closer to 20. How many anglers have had a chance to cast to, much less fight, a fish of such majesty?

But the day was not to be a disappointment—far from it. What happened during the remaining hours of daylight took much of the sting out of that major setback. At about 4:30 P.M., I experienced one of the famous Mataura evening rises that I had been hearing about since my arrival. I was walking downstream toward my rented car when I observed two fish in the center of the stream head-tail nymphing.

I stopped short, crouched low, and backed off about 75 yards away from the river. Then, still keeping low, I walked to a point about 100 yards below the working fish and cautiously eased into the river. I worked my way upstream again to where the fish had moved. To my amazement, I saw brown trout breaking the surface in all directions for 100 yards.

The feeding activity had increased when the spent wing was on the water. The fish were feeding in pairs and bobbing their heads—at the surface, under, then to the surface again. When trout stick their noses and mouths out while feeding, I call them "gulpers," and that's exactly what these babies were doing. As they fed into the current, they often came within a rod's length of me. In fact, all my prior caution was for naught, as they were virtually impossible to spook during their gulping ritual.

I was down to my last two flies, size 18 Greenwell's Glories, and the fish had become choosier even when I made direct presentations. The spent wings on the water seemed smaller, so I began thinning out the hackle on my flies. That helped. The fish were feeding so voraciously that one fish I hooked and broke off kept right on feeding with the fly still in its mouth.

I hooked nine fish, and of those I landed five and kept three. All those landed weighed between 4 and 5½ pounds.

In November and December of 1969, I was a guest of the New Zealand Government Tourist Bureau. My wife and I spent six weeks fishing both the North Island and the South Island.

The average temperature in November was 70 degrees F during the day and 55 degrees F at night. We dressed as we would if we were fishing in Montana or Wyoming in the early summer or early fall.

We discovered on our trip that when the hotels specified eating times, they meant exactly what they said. If you like to fish early and late as I do, you will have to make special arrangements or go hungry. The Takaro Lodge was the only place I found back then in all of South Island, New Zealand, that an angler or hunter could get a meal prepared any time of the day or night, even if one's tastes lean toward chateaubriand or trout à la normande.

If you are fortunate, you will experience a streamside cookout at some point during your visit. The following recipe shows how it is done, and I can see no reason why this method shouldn't work just as well back home as it does on the banks of the Mataura:

Cut and gill one trout. Wrap it in brown paper. Wrap this package in seven layers of wet newspapers and place it on hot coals. When the newspapers are dried out, the trout is done to a turn and will be almost as wonderful to eat as it was to catch.

A size 18 Greenwell's Glory dry fly lured this brown trout on New Zealand's Matura River. *Photo by Bernice Apte.*

Stu and legendary NFL Quarterback Bert Jones got into jumbo-sized redfish together. The Boga-Grips got a lot of action. *Photo by Bert Jones.*

Cajun Redfish and Cajun Quarterback

Former NFL quarterback Bert Jones throws touchdown
casts for his homeland Cajun redfish.

Bertram Hayes "Bert" Jones was born in Ruston, Louisiana. At Ruston High School, he was given the nickname "the Ruston Rifle." He went on to play quarterback for Louisiana State and then in the NFL, mostly with the Colts when they were still in Baltimore, and briefly with the Los Angeles Rams.

I fished with Bert on a number of occasions, both in the Florida Keys fly fishing for big tarpon, and on the shallow flats of the Louisiana marshes, sight fishing for Cajun redfish in 12 to 18 inches of murky water. Bert not only has great peripheral vision, but he can also cast a fly 70 or 80 feet with fantastic speed and accuracy; just as he did when throwing touchdown passes for the Colts 30 years ago.

It has been said that Bert Jones has arm strength that was rivaled only by John Elway. I would bet dollars to doughnuts that John Elway cannot come close to casting a fly or poling a skiff the way Bert Jones can.

Bert hosted Suzuki's *Great Outdoors* on the ESPN network, as well as two episodes of *The American Sportsman* on ABC with his Louisiana friend Grits Gresham. Flip Pallot and I were invited to put on two days of saltwater fly fishing seminars to a very attentive group during the second annual Fly Fishers Picnic at the Woodland Plantation, just a 40-minute drive south of New Orleans.

Bert had previously invited me to spend a couple of days at what he calls his "fish camp," redfishing in the backcountry marshes on his home waters around Port Sul-

Bert Jones shows off a highly colored Louisiana redfish.
Some believe the Cajun redfish derive their intense
coloring from the vast amounts of shrimp they eat.

fur and Venice, Louisiana, following this fly fishing picnic. When Bert decided to
join us for the last afternoon seminar and that night's banquet dinner, it gave me the
opportunity to introduce Flip to Bert.

Flip had called me about a week before the trip to ask if I would like to drive with
him, fishing our way to and from Louisiana. He had his shallow-water boat on a trail-
er behind his pickup truck and planned to spend a few days fishing along the Gulf
Coast marshes of Louisiana, Mississippi, and Alabama. Unfortunately, I already had
my plane ticket, and with the busy schedule trying to get my memoirs, *Of Wind and
Tides,* finished, I could not afford the time.

Arrangements were made for our guide, Bryan Carter, to come by the plantation at six o'clock the next morning to pick me up and have Flip follow us to the prearranged launch site where we would meet Bert Jones.

Both Flip and Bert are excellent boatmen and can pole a boat as well as any guide. So I made a command decision of having Flip and Bert fish together in Flip's boat the first day, and I would fish in Bert's boat with Bryan, because Flip had to leave the following morning, starting his drive back to Florida, and I very much wanted to get some good boat-to-boat redfish pictures.

The area we left from is adjacent to the Mississippi River, and I could see numerous weirs and dikes as we made our 40-minute run into one of Bryan's hard-to-reach secret fishing spots in the salt marsh. I had heard stories about getting dozens of casts with a fly to as many redfish, weather permitting, during an average day's fishing. In the Florida Keys, I considered getting 10 to 15 casts a good day of sight fishing redfish in the backcountry. (Although the average water clarity, except for occasionally fishing in an area inundated with mullet mud, is much better in the Florida Keys.)

Almost all the water we fished during those two days was extremely murky with mud. Even so, we were still able to see redfish sometimes 80 feet away from the boat because they were in 10 to 18 inches of water. Sometimes you'd see only a swirl or a wake, and on some occasions a red tail as the fish rooted a shrimp or crab out of the muddy bottom.

As Bryan poled the skiff in an average depth of a foot, we would see bunches of shrimps jumping out of the water. Sometimes you would see a wake created by a school of redfish slowly swimming along the shoreline, busting shrimps they shook out of the cane. The quantity of shrimps in that salt marsh was amazing, and I think you would have to see it to believe it.

When I asked Bryan whether he thought the redfish were so much more aggressive to inhaling a fly than the ones I fished for in Texas, Mississippi, and—yes—Florida because of the lack of water clarity, he replied, "I think our reds are much less spooky because of lack of boat pressure. We have more fishable habitat and more fish than anywhere else. That makes for happy redfish!"

He went on to say, "Presentation, I think, is critical to Louisiana redfishing. Get it close to them, and they tend to eat it. Short strips or long strips—as long as it's in front of them. Personally, I like crab-style flies with enough weight to give it a *hopping* action."

My analytical mind and the abundance of redfish had me experimenting with a number of flies. Using everything from a variety of bonefish patterns to chartreuse tarpon toads tied on size 1/0 Owner Aki hooks, I caught more than 40 redfish (my guide's count). Without any hesitation, I can honestly say, that was the best day of sight fishing for redfish I have ever had in my life

Most of the time, Bert and Flip would be fishing in the next marshlike lake. They were close enough for us to hear their laughter and jubilant conversation. Early on, they called us over so I could take those boat-to-boat pictures I wanted.

Our run back through the various canals with giant overhanging trees reflecting in the slick calm water made the scenic ride back to the launching ramp a photographer's dream.

Bert Jones was not only a great quarterback; he is a great fly fisherman and a great host, too, and takes a backseat to no one when it comes to cooking. We ate and were treated like royalty.

Sleep came early and fast, with dreams of catching even more Cajun redfish. I knew Bert and I were going to have another early morning of fantastic fishing with Capt. Bryan Carter, one of the great Louisiana guides. I also knew I would be back next year and the year after.

LOUISIANA REDFISH CONTACTS

CAPT. BRYAN CARTER
504-329-5198

THE UPTOWN ANGLER fly shop
Alec Griffin (manager)
504-529-3597
www.uptownangler.com

THE WOODLAND PLANTATION
21997 Highway 23
Port Sulfur, Louisiana
(a great, friendly place to stay).

Bert Jones showing off an an average Louisiana redfish
to Stu, above, and Flip Pallot, below.

Clothing still wet after being snatched out of the skiff, Stu steadies the scale as Joe Brooks looks on for the official weighing of what would go down as the largest tarpon ever caught on a fly at that time.

chapter 11

Record Tarpon: Man Overboard!

*How I was pulled overboard twice to help
Joe Brooks land his world record tarpon.*

Have you ever been pulled out of the boat by a big fish? Well, I have! Not just once but twice—in the same day.

The month was May. The year was 1961 and I was a busy fishing guide in the Lower Florida Keys. My customer was Joe Brooks, who had been my mentor since 1946, when I was only 16 years old and had set a fly rod tournament record in the Metropolitan Miami Fishing Tournament, which Joe Brooks ran as the tournament manager.

The day had been flat calm when we neared Loggerhead Bank, and I first spotted the school of about ten tarpon circling on the surface. Joe was armed with my 9-foot, 10-weight, custom-made Spinmaster fly rod and a Taurus prototype fly reel made by the Lionel Corporation. That's right, the same people who make electric trains so popular at Christmastime.

Joe had brought along his own 9½-foot Orvis Battenkill split-bamboo 9-weight, and a Fin-Nor #3 wedding cake fly reel. He wasn't using it, because a couple of hours earlier when I pulled up to a different tarpon spot, I'd inadvertently stepped on the tip of Joe's rod, breaking off about 5 inches.

That was probably the luckiest episode of the day. Joe's rod was set up with the fly tied directly to the 12-pound-test leader tippet, known as fishing "fly light." My setup, which I had brought along as a spare, had an additional 11¾ inches of 80-pound-test bite tippet between the 12-pound-test leader tippet and the fly. With my rig in his hands, Joe had considerably more firepower to cast to and deal with big fish.

Stu is intent on getting the second gaff into Joe's world record tarpon. *Photo by Joe Brooks.*

As I moved the boat slowly toward a pod of tarpon, Joe started to false cast from 100 feet to the nearest fish. In a hushed voice, I asked him to wait until I got him closer. I wanted to be in range to watch the actions of the fish as he retrieved the fly. I had my eye on two tarpon that looked considerably bigger than the rest.

About 65 feet from the nearest one on our side of the counterclockwise daisy chain, I pointed out the two largest fish and urged Joe to cast his fly slightly to the right side of the chain. I wanted his retrieve to be in the same direction the tarpon were swimming, allowing them to be the aggressors.

Joe made a perfect cast and the fly fell only a foot or so to the side and in front of the big fish's massive jaws. She went for Joe's yellow-and-orange fly at once, inhaling it. I watched as Joe struck and felt the fish, and then hit it a couple more times. That trigged the tarpon on what Joe later said was the fastest and longest run he had ever had from a fish. At the end of that run, probably 250 yards, the Taurus fly reel had maybe 40 yards of backing left. As I started my 40-horsepower engine, I suggested to Joe that he reel like he had never reeled before.

After more than an hour and 45 minutes, we were able to stay within 30 feet of the fish, allowing Joe to apply maximum pressure. Like some of the big fish often do, she started a traveling tail-beat motion, heading out to sea through a deep channel. I knew it would be now or never if we were going to land what could be a world record tarpon. I suggested to Joe that he move from the bow to the boat's cockpit. I got up on the bow with my 8-foot-long two-handed gaff.

I reached out as far as I could to embed the gaff hook into the tarpon's back. When she felt the steel, she shot forward like a torpedo, snatching me a dozen feet through the air. The gaff, which pulled clear of the fish, was still in my hands. Joe later said I looked like a pole vaulter on the way up. I came down with a big splash and hit the bottom in water neck deep. I was back in the skiff almost as fast as I had left it. Joe later remarked that I didn't even seem to touch the side of the boat as I scrambled aboard. We grinned at each other, not saying what we were both thinking: *Sharks.*

Once again we went after that great fish, and once again I had Joe *step* from the bow into the cockpit as I stepped onto the bow. This time, I again had my arms fully extended as I leaned back with all my weight when I impaled the gaff into her back.

As if in slow motion, I was once again overboard. The gaff was still in the tarpon, and the water was about chest high. I could see that she was about to rip the gaff out of her back for the second time, so I reached into the skiff, picking up my hand gaff, and stuck it into her lower jaw.

At 7 feet long and 148 pounds 8 ounces, Joe Brooks's world record tarpon outweighed my 144 pounds.

That Sunday, Vic Dunaway's column in the *Miami Herald* had a bold headline:

THE GAFF WAS A LAUGH AS THE SKIPPER TOOK A BATH.

Pulled overboard, but still hanging on to the biggest tarpon ever caught on a fly at that time, Stu is smiling and confident as he looks back at angler Joe Brooks. *Photo by Joe Brooks.*

chapter 12

"Nice Cast, Mr. President"

Harry and Bess Truman made me feel like royalty
had come on board Mom's Worry.

John Spotswood had been Monroe County's sheriff for more than a decade, and by January 1959, I had become his fair-haired boy when it came to taking dignitaries visiting Key West on fishing trips. During that time, I guided on bonefishing trips of a day or more with the U.S. Secretary of State, a commandant of the Marine Corps, head of the Florida Highway Patrol, a visiting U.S. Congressman, and Senator Estes Kefauver.

Because of Sheriff Spotswood, I found a long-term client in Bill Reynolds, president of Reynolds Metals Company (pioneers of aluminum foil), who would tie his 130-foot yacht *Intrepid* at Munson Island, locally known as Sheriff's Island. This was just off Little Torch Key, where I lived, across U.S. Highway 1 on the northwest end.

If somebody had told me when I was a young navy fighter pilot that one day I'd take a former president and First Lady out fishing, I'd have wondered what they were drinking. But that's what happened, and as the day began, I found myself worrying about proper protocol. That uneasiness went away the moment I picked up former President Harry S. Truman and Bess Truman at the *Intrepid* with my 15½-foot skiff and we started our run to the Content Keys. It was one of my favorite haunts and a spot that seemed to be home for schools of wily bonefish.

The weather was storybook perfect, and with great anticipation, I brought the skiff to a stop, tilted up my secondhand 35-horsepower Johnson outboard, and tied the boat to a 16-foot-long wooden pushpole I easily jammed into the soft mud bottom.

Now it was time for a little instruction on how to cast accurately with a spinning outfit. After a couple of "excuse me, sir" comments on his technique, I showed President Truman how to coordinate releasing the line from his first finger a fraction of time later so his shrimp would fling outward instead of straight up in the air. President Truman quickly picked up the rudiments and was casting well enough for me to start poling the boat against the incoming tide toward Content Passage. In short order, it seemed like we were almost surrounded by feeding bonefish mudding and tailing in the incoming tide.

The president's third cast was perfect, slightly upcurrent in front of a small feeding group of 6- to 7-pound bonefish. Like magic, he was hooked up to a wild fish that took off like it was shot out of cannon, screaming 100 yards of 8-pound-test monofilament from his spinning reel. I quickly pushed toward the fleeing silver bullet of a fish, but to no avail. On one of its lightning like darts, the line got wrapped around a large loggerhead sponge, creating enough additional resistance to break the line, setting the magnificent drag racer free.

President Truman uttered a curse under his breath as he turn toward me, asking what happened.

Twenty minutes later, that same scenario was repeated like déjà vu. When Mrs. Truman softly, almost shyly looked toward me, she asked, "Captain, what does a lady do when a lady, er, has to go?"

"Well, ma'am, I could put you on that little beach on West Content Key," I replied, pointing to that area, "but the mosquitoes, deer flies, and no-see-ums would certainly try feasting on your tender flesh. Or I could run you back to my house on Little Torch Key, but we would lose about two hours of this prime bonefish tide."

President Truman quickly interjected, "Oh no, those two fish hooked me and I want to catch at least one bonefish today."

Walking by Mrs. Truman, I lifted the lid on my live-bait tank in the back of the boat, just behind the cockpit, exposing the live shrimps and holes in the bottom of the boat, and politely said, "Well, ma'am, I have had other ladies . . ."

Without any other words, she looked me right in the eye, saying, "I understand, Captain. Both of you gentlemen go to the front of the boat, whistle, sing, or splash water—just make noise."

That day, President Truman hooked four more bonefish, landing two of them before the tide changed and we ran back to the *Intrepid,* ending a fantastic few hours of fishing for a great president.

It had been a dreamlike great honor for me that ended with a hearty handshake.

Did you know that President Harry S. Truman was the only president in the 20th century without a college degree? That he was the son of a Missouri farmer and served five years in the national guard, then volunteered to serve at age 33 after World War I broke out, even though he was two years over the draft age and exempt as a farmer. He became a captain in a field artillery unit, serving in the fighting in the Meuse-Argonne. Yes, I was privileged and honored to take President Harry S. and Mrs. Truman bonefishing.

A big, toothy barracuda like this one goes after prey with speed and power. The chartreuse tube lure proves once again: "If it ain't chartreuse, it ain't no use." *Photo by Pat Ford.*

Barracuda: The Tiger That Swims

They terrorize other fish but can make an angler's day.
Wherever it swims, the barracuda is a fish to be reckoned with.

Anglers are generally pretty good about picking nicknames for their favorite fish. Take the barracuda. The "tiger of the sea," as it's known, has a ferocious appearance and an awesome set of teeth, plus the mystery and stealth necessary to emulate its jungle namesake. I've often wondered why they don't call real tigers the "barracudas of the jungle." As a predator, the 'cuda can be equal to anything on earth, or in the sea.

As a game fish, the barracuda reaches just as high a pinnacle. Often known as the "saber-toothed bonefish," it will give almost as big a thrill on its first run as the legendary gray ghost of the flats. Then, as an added bonus, it will startle you with a greyhound leap for a punctuation mark.

No bonefish will do that!

The barracuda, in fact, has saved many a fishing guide from having an embarrassing day, including yours truly. After a hard day of chasing uncooperative bonefish, barracudas can provide the action the client has paid for.

It is a hard-fighting, elusive, determined target, with intelligence, speed, and uncommonly good eyesight that can make you work hard to score. And its glistening teeth command a respect not many other game fish are given. But for all that, barracudas are readily available, and can be caught, if you know how. Like many other champions, the 'cuda has a weakness. And that is its fondness for a fast-moving tube lure.

A tube lure is merely a piece of surgical tubing 12 to 14 inches long, with a treble hook at the tail end. I prefer to use either chartreuse or orange tubing; it is particularly sure-fire to take barracuda. To make a tube lure, just thread a wire leader through the tubing, add a treble hook at the far end and a swivel, with or without a ¼-ounce sinker, at the head. It's ready to tie on to a wire leader, and on the flats, just pick out the fish you want to cast to.

The best way to operate a tube lure is to make a long cast beyond the barracuda, in front of it. With your rod tip held high, retrieve it as fast as possible, bringing the lure past your quarry. It is impossible for you to outrun the fish with your lure, because of the 'cuda's blinding speed. But the extremely fast action will provoke a strike.

The tube lure probably looks like a needlefish, or houndfish, to the barracuda, and the very fast retrieve makes it seem like the prey is trying to escape, or that it is chasing another fish. Whatever, the 'cuda is suddenly interested.

Sight fishing and presenting the lure right to the fish is the ultimate fun of flats fishing. But fishing the reefs with a tube lure can be productive also. The main difference is you will be mostly making long blind casts, and you will seldom see your quarry ahead of time.

On the reefs, where the barracudas lie in wait for other fish to provide them a meal, they may not be so active as they are on the flats. That calls for another technique to get them excited enough to strike. It's called teasing.

To tease a barracuda from among the schools that might just be hanging around, rig a live bait of almost any kind—blue runner, pinfish, snapper, or yellowtail—onto the end of a strong line. Cast among the barracudas, and retrieve rapidly. At least one of the fish will surely follow it back to the boat. Bring the teaser bait alongside and, keeping it just at the surface, make it splash and squirm. The barracudas will turn on it almost immediately and make a try for the teaser bait. Snatch the teaser out of the water and then back onto the surface so that it starts splashing again. You have to be quick because the barracuda's lunge can be like lightning.

The barracuda can be driven frantic with this offer-and-denial method. Now, cast your tube lure to the fish you have chosen—and hang on. If, because of their superior eyesight, they have refused your tube lure, the teasing will provoke them into forgetting about caution and murdering your lure.

Facing. A 38-pound barracuda that Capt. Bob Montgomery has on a lip gaff for Stu. This 'cuda is a fly-rod world record on 12-pound-class tippet.

When people are snorkeling or scuba diving and are unfamiliar with their surroundings, they sometimes become unnecessarily spooked by the presence of these fish. A barracuda is so curious about what things are in its world that it will come close and stare, grinning amiably all the while. When a swimmer drops over the side of the boat, a barracuda will close in, just out of range, and give him the once-over. If the swimmer moves toward the fish, it will move away, keeping its distance, but if the swimmer backpedals, the 'cuda will simply follow along at the same arm's length, watching. I have also seen them swimming alongside my skiff, apparently just looking to see what I was doing. The minute they saw me raise an arm to cast, however, they were gone.

A really big barracuda—5 feet long and 40 or more pounds—honestly deserves the title "great barracuda," but I think its reputation for savagery, unprovoked, is ill earned. That is not to say, of course, that there have not been attacks. Even a barracuda attack by mistake is not a pretty sight.

A scuba diver who spears a barracuda may expect to be severely dealt with by a wounded tiger of the sea. They can be very unforgiving.

But just as vulnerable is the angler who brings a snapping set of of barracuda teeth aboard his boat. Many hapless fishermen have received nasty bites that way. There was a case in Biscayne Bay when a Pan American airlines pilot was severely bitten on the leg by a hooked saber-tooth that leaped aboard his boat while he was fighting it.

Barracudas on the flats range from little ones I call "hooda-cudas," at 2 or 3 pounds, on up to 25- and 30-pounders. In the shallow water, a hooked 'cuda seems to go into a state of panic, with nowhere to hide. It will give you a terrific aerial display, but they do fight more like a bonefish, making multiple runs. They're so fast, you cannot follow them. They will drag your line in one direction and suddenly appear, airborne, way off to the other side of where you thought they were. They are so hard to locate when they are panicked. That's why there are very few good photographs of jumping barracudas.

Barracudas on the reefs aren't nearly such hard fighters as the same fish on the shallow flats. They might make only one or two zippy runs, maybe jump a couple of times, then just dog it as you try to force them in. Still, it's a good place to catch big ones, and can be a fine place for fly fishing. One of my biggest on a fly was a 31-pounder, caught off Key West.

It was early January, not long after a cold front had passed. The water conditions were excellent. It was sunny, calm, and clear. The barracudas were "showering" schools of ballyhoo. That is, bunching them up in tight little balls, so the baitfish were jumping wildly out of the water in a desperate escape attempt. Using a ballyhoo-type fly made of nylon, tensile, and bucktail, I made a long cast into the actively feeding predators and started stripping line to move the fly as fast as I could. The big barracuda hit it like a freight train, smashing my fly with a vengeance.

I set the hook, and after a tough but quick fight brought it to gaff. This 31-pounder became the IGFA 12-pound-class-tippet fly record, but was only one of six barracudas I caught that day that exceeded 20 pounds, taken over a reef in approximately 60 feet of water.

The barracuda is, to my thinking, strictly a sport fish: Unless you intend to mount a spectacular specimen because it is a world record, it should always be released, never killed. They are too fine a game fish to kill, just for the sake of dockside bragging.

If jungle tigers ran in packs the way barracudas sometimes do, nothing in India would be safe.

Roaming the flats like a tiger, the barracuda will attack ballyhoo-like streamers as viciously as it does tube lures. *Photo by Pat Ford.*

The fly rod was Ted Williams' favorite wand for flats fishing, but he used spinning tackle when conditions warranted it. Here he shows off a beautiful bonefish, with Stu on the pushpole.

chapter 14

Snook and the Slugger

My Ted Williams adventures lasted many years with tarpon,
bonefish, and others. But snook was the fish that first brought
the most famous hitter in baseball to my door.

You cut a freshman college class to go fishing. What happens? Does fate punish you? No! You end up meeting Ted Williams.

A chance meeting brought me together with Ted Williams in the late fall of 1948. At the time, I was attending the University of Miami as a freshman and had cut a three-hour Botany lab, my only class that day, to spend the first of several days fishing for snook in the canals alongside U.S. Route 41 (US 41) leading to Naples.

It was an overcast, blustery fall day in South Florida, just cool enough to keep the mosquito population from being too active. I left my house in Miami around three o'clock in the morning and drove down US 41—also known as the Tamiami Trail—to the Marco Canal area in order to arrive by daybreak. I'd heard that jumbo-size snook had been cruising the incoming tide, looking for a meal.

After what I considered a very successful morning's fly fishing, having caught four nice snook over 10 pounds and two of them easily over 15, I headed back toward the Tamiami Trail to see if any of the schools of smaller snook were busting the minnows along the runoffs from the Everglades.

I drove a 1941 De Soto that had seen better years. My fly rod poked out the left rear window, waving in the wind as I cruised along at 45 miles an hour, looking for feeding fish.

After driving 10 to 15 miles, I didn't see any indication of snook chasing minnows on the far bank. Then, a flurry of feeding fish busted loose in one of my favorite places. Pulling over to the side of the road, I jumped out almost before Betsy came to a full stop. You have to be quick in order to get a fly to these fish while they're still feeding, before they move on. Well, I was quick but not quick enough, and by the time I got a fly line stripped off the reel, they were gone. I stood for a while looking, but to no avail. I wound in my fly line, hooked my popping bug on a snake guide, and wrapped the loose line around my reel so I could dash into action if I found more fish down the road.

Five miles farther down the road, I saw a guy casting a fly, so I pulled over to watch. In no time at all, it became obvious to me that he knew what to do with his fly rod. I got out of Betsy, carefully walking behind him and over to his left side, making sure I wouldn't hinder his casting.

After watching him make beautiful presentations to the far bank of the canal, I asked, "Having any luck?"

He neither responded nor acknowledged my presence, not even glancing toward me. I stood there watching while he made three or four more casts and thinking that maybe he's so engrossed in casting that he didn't hear me.

"Have you caught any snook yet today?" I queried, this time a little louder; he might be hearing impaired.

It seemed obvious that with the mention of the word "snook," he figured I wasn't just some tourist driving toward Miami and trying to pass the time of day while stretching my legs. Without so much as interrupting the cadence of his cast or turning toward me even a little, he replied, "And just what do you know about snook?"

Being a little feisty myself, I self-assuredly responded, "I know enough about snook that I caught four this morning over ten pounds each, and two over fifteen."

That stopped him cold in his tracks. He half turned toward me, his eyes examining me for the first time. Now I definitely had his complete attention. "And just where on this earth did you do that?"

For the first time he notices the fly rod sticking out of Betsy's back window and my Dade County, Florida, license tag. "In the Marco Canal," I said.

"Yeah, then what the hell are you doing over here?" he answered sharply, as if disbelieving my assertion.

"The big cruisers that we spot swimming along before we cast our fly to them move only a few hours after daybreak," I replied. "And it's after daybreak."

The man now realized I wasn't just making up tall tales about catching snook, and that indeed he must be in the know about snook fishing in these parts. As he wound in his fly line, he coyly asked, "Where is this fantastic place in the Marco Canal?"

"I've never checked the mileage on my odometer, and it would be difficult to describe the spot with so many curves and areas that look alike," I replied. "But I plan on going back there tomorrow morning for a few hours after daybreak before returning to Miami. You're welcome to meet me in the parking area at Royal Palm Hammock on the cut-off to Marco from US 41 at, say, six A.M., and we'll catch daybreak where we're going to fish."

I didn't know this guy from Adam, but I was thinking it would be nice having company, especially someone who cast a fly like this big dude did.

"Where you staying tonight?" he asked.

"I'll be sleeping in old Betsy," I said as I waved my arm toward the old De Soto, "in the Royal Palm Hammock parking area."

"Are the mosquitoes pretty bad during the night?"

"Yep," I replied. "But I have plenty of mosquito dope, and it's cool enough to only leave one window cracked an inch."

He answered immediately. "I'm staying at Weavers Camp just a few miles up the road, and only twenty minutes' drive that time of the morning," he said while slowly walking to his station wagon. "See you at six A.M., sharp." He emphasized "sharp" loudly, as if he were a drill sergeant.

"Boy, wish I could afford to stay at Weavers Camp," I mumbled to myself.

Five forty-five the next morning seemed to come around all too fast. Curled up on the backseat and wrapped in a blanket, I awoke with someone rudely knocking on my window and a bright flashlight shining in my face. It scared the shit out of me for a moment. I reached for my .22 pistol on the floor but stopped when I realized the time and who was probably rousting me out of a deep sleep.

After uncovering from my blanket, sitting up yawning and stretching, I unlocked the door and stepped out into the dark morning. My wristwatch said ten minutes to six, and I quickly thought, this fucking big dude sure was anxious as all get-out. But the words that instead came out of my mouth showed no anger.

"Good morning," I said, "you're right on time to do battle with some big linesides." Snook, with the long, dark lateral lines across the length of their bodies, are sometimes called such.

The new dawn was already showing in the eastern sky. "Let's go," he said. "I'll follow you with my car." He walked over and got into his station wagon, engine still running.

I loved to fish as much as anybody, but couldn't help but muse once more that this fellow sure seemed damn anxious to tangle with a big one that morning. The least he could have done was brought me a doughnut or cup of coffee. I climbed into the front seat, started Betsy's engine, and headed out of the parking area to the Marco Road.

Twenty minutes later, it was light enough for me to recognize where I wanted to pull off the road and wait for the cruisers to show.

Not wanting to waste any time, I quickly started assembling my two-piece fly rod. Having left it rigged, all I needed to do now was line up the guides, push the ferrules together, pull some fly line off the reel, and make sure my hook on the fly was still sharp. I was ready.

Looking back at the big guy's station wagon, I could see that he was doing about the same.

Fishing that morning was almost as good as the previous day. I caught only two, and my newfound friend managed to out-fish me, catching three nice snook, all over 10 pounds. His biggest looked to be a good solid 15 pounds while both my fish weighed at least 15 pounds.

The flow of cruisers coming in with the current stopped just as quickly as it had started. It seemed like in no time at all, my watch said 10:30. The action was over. Time to get ready for the 70-mile drive home.

While I was disassembling my rod and putting the tackle away, the tall one walked up with a piece of paper in his left hand and his right hand extended, casually saying, "My name is Ted Williams. What's yours?"

After telling him, he says, "I sure enjoyed fishing with you, Bush. My phone number in Coral Gables is on this piece of paper. Give me a call next time you're going fishing."

With that, we went our own ways.

Not being a baseball fan to the point that I hardly even knew the Boston Red Sox existed, I had no idea Ted Williams was anything but just another guy who knew what do with a fly rod. And so began a friendship that lasted more than 40 years.

One afternoon a month later when I got home from classes at the University of Miami, my mother greeted me. "Some man by the name of Ted Williams called three times today, leaving his phone number each time. And his last call, he sounded a little agitated that you had not returned his calls."

"Mom, I don't know a Ted Williams," I said.

"He claims to have fished with you on the Marco Canal and had some good snook fishing," Mother replied.

"Oh, that big dude," I remarked, the memory coming back. First I put the books in my bedroom, changed out of my college clothes into something more comfortable, and still not knowing that Ted Williams was anything special other than a big guy who cast a good fly line, I called him.

The phone rang so many times that I nearly hung up. A lady's voice finally answered, "Williams residence."

"Is Ted Williams in?" I asked.

"Um, I'll have to look and see," she answered wearily. "Who's calling, please?"

"Please tell him it's Stu Apte, returning his call."

"Stu who?" she asked, the first of many, many times those words were to be uttered on the phone. For some reason, that's the response I usually got when calling, and just for grins I decided to put that on future license plates: STU WHO?

"Just tell him the Stu he fished with at the Marco Canal."

Waiting at least five minutes, I was again getting impatient and close to hanging up before I hear a man's voice. "Stu, I was in the middle of tying a bonefish fly, sorry you had to wait." Without hardly taking a breath, he asked, "There is a great wading tide for bonefish tomorrow—you want to go?"

Short and sweet—no small talk—right to the point. I soon came to recognize that this was "Ted talk," with just the important things said. Luckily, with only three classes each week, the next day was free.

"Sure," said I. "Where do you plan on going?"

"I store my skiff in a warehouse on the water in Coconut Grove. It'll be a short run from there across Biscayne Bay to Soldier Key."

Following his lead of no idle chitchat, I asked what time he wanted me there. Again, I still did not have the slightest inkling who Ted Williams was.

Ted said, "How about eight o'clock? There's an outgoing tide until just after ten, so we'll be able to catch the last hour of the outgoing tide and the important first couple of hours of the incoming tide. That will give us the best fishing for tailing bonefish."

"Sounds good to me—what can I bring?" I asked. "Lunch?"

"... he's one helluva fine fly fisherman."

"No, Bush, I'll have everything we need. See you at eight o'clock, and be on time."

"Don't worry about that, and thanks." Now I was beginning to wonder why in the hell he kept calling me Bush.

That evening, Bill Lewis, a fishing friend and classmate, called asking if I wanted to go snook fishing tomorrow. I casually informed him that I was going bonefishing at Soldier Key with some big dude I had met last month while snook fishing on the Marco Canal. "I gotta tell you, Bill, he's one helluva fine fly fisherman."

"Yeah? What's his name, maybe I know him?"

"Ted Williams," I replied. Almost before I got the words out of my mouth, Bill almost sucked all the air out of my ear through the phone, "Holy shit, do you mean Ted Williams, the Ted Williams, the great Boston Red Sox baseball player?"

"Damned if I know if that's the same guy," I replied. "But now that you mention it, I did notice that he has a Massachusetts license tag on his station wagon. I'll probably find out tomorrow and will let you know."

And that was the first inkling of just who this big dude actually was.

I am not ashamed to say that Ted out-fished me that day, catching three bonefish for each of mine. We managed to stay out of each other's way, helping each other when needed, and started the bonding of a lifelong friendship.

Our friendship had to be put on hold during the time I was going to Mexico City College from 1950 to 1951, and when Ted was called back into the Marine Corps as a fighter pilot in 1952.

During his Marine Corps stint, a navy flight surgeon who was Ted's marine air wing's flight surgeon in Korea became the flight surgeon for my air group at NAAS Oceana, Virginia, in 1953. The first time I met him in sick bay, he said, "Hmm, Ensign Stuart Apte . . . can you be the same person Ted Williams talked about while I was his air wing flight surgeon in Korea?"

Before I could answer, he asked, "Did you and Ted do a lot of fishing together?"

I told him that I was indeed that man. "Small damn world we live in," he said with a head shake. "Ted mentioned he heard a younger fishing buddy of his was a naval aviator, a fellow fighter pilot, and to keep an eye out for him. Can't believe I actually ran into you."

Yes, a small world indeed. As a matter of fact, not many people know this, but while in Korea, Ted served as the wingman on numerous missions with future astronaut and U.S. Senator John Glenn.

Papa Pours a Batch

When Papa Hemingway whips up a batch of his famous
mojito cocktails, look out for the deck to start spinning.

The year was 1957, and I was in Havana, visiting an American friend, Mike Brandon, whose wealthy parents owned a clothing manufacturing business and a chain of Mini Max Supermarkets throughout Cuba. Their beautiful home was in a gated community called Country Club Palace, situated in an exclusive residential part of Havana. They were members of the Havana Yacht Club, and Mike enjoyed taking visitors from the United States there to look over the big yachts, large fancy fishing boats, and to partake in an expensive but fantastic lunch.

After having lunch with me one day at the club, Mike was invited to go somewhere with a very pretty young lady. He asked if I would mind fending for myself for an hour or so. I told him no problem, and that I'd spend a couple of hours strolling along the docks, looking at the boats, the big tarpon rolling in the harbor and the multitude of fish alongside the docks waiting for handouts.

"See you later." Mike said, glancing back over his shoulder as he and his lady friend briskly walked off, holding hands.

I've had good reason to believe that most things in my life seem to happen for a good reason, and once again I was about to experience one of those happenings. It was around two o'clock, there was very little activity on the boats that were tied up at the dock, and I was thoroughly enjoying my walk while reading their interesting names and admiring all the fish swimming alongside them.

Walking up to a boat with a name that seemed vaguely familiar—*Pilar*—I politely asked the gentleman sitting on the lone fighting chair if he had been out fishing lately. I had no idea I was speaking to Ernest Hemingway.

"You're an American, huh? And you like to fish," he said whimsically.

"Yes, sir, I'm a part-time fishing guide in the Florida Keys and a part-time pilot for Pan American World Airways," I answered.

"Well, Mr. Fishing Guide . . . Pilot . . . come aboard and join me for a mojito." He gestured for me to go aboard.

Taking my shoes off before stepping onto the gunwale and into the cockpit area, I asked, "Thank you for inviting me on board for a, uh, mo—, mo— What did you call that drink?"

"You're welcome, young man, it's merely a Cuban mint julep, and it's pronounced *moe-HEE-toe*," he said.

Cuban mint julep indeed, I thought, *what will they think of next?* Truthfully, I don't know how many mojito drinks we polished off while talking fishing and fully agreeing on fish-fighting techniques during the next few hours.

And a real shock came when he said he knew my name and guiding reputation from reading some of the numerous Sunday columns of Alan Carson and then Vic Dunaway, the new outdoor editor of the *Miami Herald,* who wrote about my successful guiding out of Little Torch Key.

After Mike Brandon came walking along the dock, looking for me, and my doing a slurred introduction, I required a little dockside help to leave *Pilar.*

I later found out Ernest Hemingway would make the Cuban mojito almost as famous as the running of the bulls in Pamplona.

This is how Papa Hemingway made them: Put 4 to 12 mint leaves with stems in a highball glass; add 1 teaspoon powdered sugar and about 2 ounces of club soda. Thoroughly crush the mint leaves until you get the mint aroma. Add two ounces of good white rum, two ounces fresh-squeezed key lime juice, fill the glass with crushed ice, and stir in club soda to taste. Use a sprig of mint as garnish.

Sit back with a fishing friend and discuss the pros and cons of the various ways to land big fish quickly. The only thing you won't have is the one and only Ernest Hemingway mixing them for you.

Papa Hemingway named his fishing boat Pilar *for the daughter he always wanted but never had. When he took delivery of his new boat, he had the Spanish name painted on. Later, the name Pilar became known internationally when Hemingway used it for one of the major characters in his big novel* For Whom the Bell Tolls.

chapter 16

Irish Salmon—With an Audience

*I wasn't prepared for the test I faced when I put my "Yank"
techniques and gear to work on Atlantic salmon in Ireland.*

The idea of a crowd took me by surprise. I wasn't used to performing before a
gallery. And this wasn't a golf course; it was a "beat" on a swift-moving river at
Castle Connell, in Ireland. The local folks had come to watch "the Yank" fish
for big Atlantic salmon with a fly rod more suited, they thought, for wee brown
trout. Some hoped I could; others wanted me to stub my toe.

I was thinking of all this as I rigged my slender 7½-foot bamboo rod, a handmade
present from renowned rod builder Nat Uslan.

"Sure," came a thick Irish brogue, "if ye should be lucky enuf to reach the lie, and if
ye should be lucky enuf to have a salmon take yer fly, ye'd not be lucky enuf to handle
him wit that wee little rod!" The gallery guffawed, for this man was one of the best
gillies in all of County Limerick, Ireland.

Another sang out, "An' what size leader ye be usin', pray?" I told him that it was
tapered down to a 7½-pound tippet. More laughter.

"Well, ye should know we use a straight 25-pound leader here, with a two-handed
spay rod, fit fer a man. Ye'll nivver be able to keep him from the rapids, where he'll
surely break off!" I couldn't help smiling to myself.

The crowd roared again as I made ready to cast. But then a sharp voice said, "Quiet!
Let him fish." It was Lord Daresbury, and immediately there was silence. I was his
guest.

Above and facing. As an Irish audience looks on, Stu manages to probe the Atlantic salmon lies with tackle the locals had never seen used for salmon— a 7 ½ foot Nat Uslan split cane trout rod. *Photo by Bernice Apte.*

Lord Daresbury was a tall, offbeat, unstuffy type, but you knew right away he was in command. Old British aristocracy, dating back to William the Conqueror, with an estate half the size of Rhode Island. He was Master of the Hunt for all Ireland, with a stable of 65 specially bred English hunter-jumpers and a kennel of 250 prized hounds whose pedigrees registered a hundred generations. For all his dignity, he had a rare wit and loved a good wager. His passions were riding to the hounds, and fishing.

But, like everything Lord Daresbury did, there was a personal rule, a narrowly confined limit that controlled all: fairness.

I had been a Pan Am pilot, but was making a living then as a fishing guide out of Little Torch Key, 28 miles northeast of Key West, Florida, poling a backcountry skiff, sweating in the tropic sun, loving every minute of it, finding fish for my clients. They were a mix of average to wealthy, and Lord Daresbury topped the list.

One of the fortunate rich, he could afford to spend every winter fishing Cozumel, Yucatán, then March and April in the Keys, before traveling home for the mayfly hatch in Ireland.

Toby—he allowed only a few intimates to use his first name (I don't know what his wife, Lady Hilton-Green, called him, but he called her Boodeley)—loved sight fishing for bonefish, but considered trout fishing with wet flies beneath his dignity, as unfair advantage. He did enjoy watching me challenge hundred-pound tarpon on the fly, however, and often invited me to spend some time at his estate in Ireland, if I was ever "in the vicinity."

My chance came sooner than I'd expected. Pan Am called me back to fly overseas routes. So I made arrangements to fish that famous mayfly hatch, on Toby's Irish river, the Camogue.

Stu and Lord Tony Terry pose for a picture.
Photo by Bernice Apte.

The lord's footman met my Pan Am flight in a Rolls, not a carriage. Daresbury's marvelous estate was just out of Shannon, in County Limerick, among the emerald green hills of Ireland. Bathed in spring light, even the pale overcast sky glowed with a soft green tinge, as if at any moment, it would spawn a gaggle of shamrocks and leprechauns.

Daresbury House was huge, looming over the verdant hills, master of all it surveyed. My bedroom was half the size of my entire home in the Florida Keys. But nothing is perfect: It was icy cold. And central heating was all but unknown in the Emerald Isle. Instead, they had roaring fireplaces and heated stones wrapped in blankets to warm the beds at night.

I wasn't sure how to act in these regal surroundings, but having heard the British always dressed for dinner, I struggled into a suit. Then I stood among the liveried butlers and footmen in the vast dining room with a table as big as a soccer field, awaiting . . . Toby.

He swept in, casually dressed in a sweatsuit. He had been doing laundry. His wife, Lady Hilton-Green, was off to Paris with some of her prized horses entered into the steeplechase, so Lord Daresbury was compelled to use his private Laundromat himself; he didn't trust the maids with machines.

We dined on a huge roast of beef, pheasant, and asparagus grown in his private garden. It showed me another, even friendlier side of the lord. While I cut up the succulent stalks of asparagus and dipped them in butter sauce with my fork, I glanced up at him. Toby simply plucked up a whole stem, sloshed it in butter, and then almost inhaled it whole, like a large brown trout, I thought.

It was then he told me I would fish the Camogue, at a beat his mother used to fish daily, with flies made for her by the Hardy Brothers, Britain's outfitters to royalty. But first I had a date on a neighbor's river, at Castle Connell.

I would fish. He would watch. Role reversal, sure, but Lord Daresbury did not fish for salmon, which would not take dry flies in this river and allow him to exercise his dry fly fishing skill. Wet flies were unfair advantage. He called them "chukka-chance" or likened the use of them to fishing in a boot. He was so dead set against wet flies, he would not let anyone fish his private river with them for fear they would take all the fish. Only one friend, his personal physician, was an exception, because Toby figured the doctor was a very poor angler, and he made house calls.

So he had set me up with his friend Lord Tony Terry, who had asked a British duke to give up a day so the Yank who caught monsters on trout gear could try a really tough fish, the Atlantic salmon. That pulled the gallery; the word had got around.

I cast across the pool and reached the lie with no trouble. No takes. By the 25th cast, the crowd was beginning to rumble, and suddenly my line stopped, as though snagged. I tightened up, and the fish moved. I hit it two, three, four times. It surged away. It was tough, strong, but nothing like a tarpon. No match for proper fish-fighting techniques, even with my little rod. Quickly I dominated it, never letting it leave the pool, and soon had it lying there, gleaming silver, puffing, thoroughly whipped. It was 19½ pounds. The time was 13 minutes. My first Atlantic salmon.

I heard grumbles behind me. "Lucky," someone said. I turned to watch, and about half the gallery was paying off the other half. It seems Irishmen like a slight wager, even on fishing. Some had taken the odds and backed the Yank. I grinned, offering the salmon to my host, Lord Daresbury, who would present it to Lord Terry. Protocol.

"Yes, yes," he said, very pleased. "If one of you gillies would split this thing down the middle, I'll give Lord Terry his due." Apparently, he had challenged the Lord Terry to let the Yank fish. If I scored big, he got to keep half the salmon.

"I knew you couldn't miss, my boy," he told me. "After all, he does allow wet flies. It was," he chuckled, "chukka-chance."

Barramundi with one of Stu's classy streamer flies in its mouth.

Creatures of the Night "Down Under"

Crocs, poison snakes, 8-inch bugs—and trophy barramundi!
They're all on the agenda in Australia's trackless wild.

It was the first time in ten days that I had seen John "Digger" Entcastle pull on his boots. "Barefoot was better," he had insisted—through foreign trees, gravel, and river mud. I stood there, fully booted as usual, and wondered why he was suddenly booting up.

"It's the geechies," he said, "These little black snakes. They're all about, you know, where we're fishing today." He grinned. "Poison. Deadly. The boots are for stomping 'em, awright?"

We were far back in the trackless wilderness northwest of Cairns, Australia, on one of Queensland's wild rivers, to fish for barramundi on light tackle. Our group included John, a sugarcane farmer, outfitter Jack Erskine, and renowned Australian writer John Matera.

I've been met all over the world by an assortment of interesting characters, but these Aussies were a macho lot—so superhuman, they never would show fear, and always up for a good dare.

Queensland was the place to bring out the Aussie spirit. We had supplies for two weeks, including tents and fishing gear. We had four-wheeled it through the bush country on animal trails, past roving herds of wallabies and wild pigs, and hundreds of unnamed birds. Everything Down Under takes a different look. All are rare species to an outlander. It was truly like another world, all around me.

There was no way out but the way we'd come, unless by chance you found a ranch house. And there was one, in fact, 25 miles from us; with nobody home. The owners had gone to drive cattle to Cooktown. This ranch stretched 100 square miles.

We arrived in black dark and parked the lorry on a steep rise over the lagoon. It took an hour to set up camp and stuff down a bit of mutton, and I was ready to wash off the grime before hitting the sack. I grabbed my gear and headed for the lagoon.

Down there, I swung the lantern around. Not much brush, muddy lagoon banks, with a few particular slick areas about 3 feet wide, leading right into the water, which was welcome, even if it was warm and dark as the Okefenokee Swamp. I stripped down, dropped the bucket, then hoisted it to pour over my head.

Wonderful. I soaked up, feeling better already. Time to hit the sack. I started to give the bucket a heave to fill up for a final soaking.

"No! No! Not there. Go down fifty paces!" It was Jack Erskine, shouting from his tent. I thought he had gone right off to sleep.

"Why not?" I said.

"It's the crocs. Big, salty ones, twenty feet long, some o' them. The first time you dip the bucket in, they locate you. The next time, they're waiting just under to drag you in. They can up and grab a full-grown horse and rider in an eyeblink."

A chill raced up my spine as I realized what those mudslides along the bank were. Cautiously I gathered my gear, stepped back half a dozen paces, and moved down 100 yards to rinse.

A week before, Digger told me gleefully, a big croc had broken a horse's neck and threw it 20 feet from the bank. The rider escaped. Next day, they found half a cow hidden under a deadfall in the river. The crocs are ravenous, and vicious, too.

I didn't sleep well, if at all, the first night, a stranger in a strange land, deep in a forest whose trees I didn't know, with crocs, and with snakes I couldn't see or identify, full of poison. I'm not a fearful type, far from it, but I don't like threatening reptiles of any size. These fearless Aussies were a special breed. I held them in awe.

As the days wore on, we fished numerous areas, caught dozens of barramundi, and saw more of Australia's wilderness rivers and lagoons, not to mention more crocodiles.

Barramundi are fine game fish, 10 to 30 pounds, a lot like our snook, without the predominant stripe down the side. They fight like snook, seldom jump, but have great strong runs, and try to wrap around deadfalls and stumps to break you off. Skinned out, they have the same sweet soapy smell, and cooked they taste like snook. Great!

Facing. Stu showing friend Jack Erskine
the barramundi taken on a lure.

This barra went for a top water plug worked in "walking-the-dog" fashion.

The "barra," as the Aussies call them, have a very strong strike, one you can actually hear as well as feel, underwater. Digger caught the first one as I stood next to him, and I heard the distinct *blopp* when it hit. That's a hell of an inhale.

I never quite got used to the crocodiles enough to match the Aussies. Digger would not admit fright if his hair were standing straight up. I truly envied him.

One night, fishing a dark lagoon surrounded by rocks, brush, and the ever-present mudslides, I felt chills running up my back once more. I could hear big splashes into the water and roughly in the brush quite a bit higher than in the path we had to take back to camp. I knew they were near, waiting.

Midnight rolled by, we had fished enough, had a good catch, and started back along the path. Then the last flashlight, inexplicably went out. We would have to move in the dim moonlight following the faintly outlined head of the man in front.

Every shutter of the brush put us on edge, but it was the loud crashing of a body hurling between John and me that made us both jump straight up in the air. I yelled, "Look out!" But in a second, it was past. And immediately we could smell what had made the commotion.

Not a 20-foot crocodile. A small herd of wild pigs we had startled from their beds. They can slice you up, but even a 20-pound porker will run if you don't corner it.

"All right, lads, it was only a pig," Digger cooed. "P'raps I'd better lead us back to camp, before you lose ten years to your fear o' the pig!" He laughed. We continued down the path.

An hour later, a few drinks, and a lot of laughs from Digger's ribbing, I fell quickly asleep. But Queensland had a final jab in the ribs for me.

I awakened suddenly in the pitch black as something large and heavy thumped onto my chest. Something alive! I threw up the cover, too startled to yell, and it hit the floor. Pulse pounding in my ears, I splashed the flashlight beam on my attacker.

There crawled the biggest rhinoceros beetle in creation. I've seen them in Guyanese and Costa Rican jungles, but this one—an incredible 8 inches long, with a pincer that would have made a 5-pound lobster proud. It scuttled away from the light, and I sank back, thankful I had not awakened the others with a bug scare. But my dreams didn't last.

In minutes, the beetle was back on my chest. It must have weighed a full pound. I thrashed at it again, flinging it away, but this time the monster caromed off the tent wall and landed squarely on Digger's neck. From a sound sleep, he came straight up off the bed, yelling, "Get it off! Get it the hell off me!" Wild eyed, he was truly panicked.

I jumped up, flashed the light on the beetle, and slapped it down. This time I nudged it out of the tent flap. I turned to Digger. The veins in his neck were pumping like an oil derrick. "It's okay, lad," I said, "go back to sleep. It was only a bug."

It was my turn to smile and clamp him on the shoulder. Digger Entcastle was, after all, only human.

He might have relaxed at that. I'll never know. For the first time in ten days, I slept like a log.

The gang's all here for an episode for *The American Sportsmen*.
Actor Jason Miller ("The Exorcist") is on the left with Curt Gowdy,
and Stu is on the right chatting with the lodge owner.

chapter 18

Curt Gowdy: The American Sportsman

Just to know him was a gift. To fish with him was a treasure.

One of my favorite memories of Curt Gowdy was when we were doing an *American Sportsman* show in Costa Rica in 1977. Curt and I were cohosting the show at Isla de Pesca, a new fishing lodge on the Colorado River in the northern Caribbean part of Costa Rica.

Wh
hile we were walking through an overgrown, dank, dark jungle path in order to get to a portion of beach that I wanted to wade-fish for snook, Curt turned to me and asked, "Are there any snakes in this part of the jungle?"

"Only fer-de-lance and bushmasters," I replied, naming two of the deadliest.

Curt almost jumped out of his skin, but he pressed on, going fishing.

A few days before we arrived in Costa Rica, there had been a storm with a tremendous amount of rain that brought large trees floating out of the river into the now-coffee-colored water. That made the fishing for snook extremely difficult, but being the good sport that he was, Curt waded out into the riled water pockmarked with large pieces of timber rolling in the surf.

We caught only a couple of snook in that portion of the show, but it was great sitting on a large log, listening to him talk about his thoughts on why some of us die-hards fish.

When he was asked how he started fishing, he said that his dad started teaching him when he was ten years old, fishing for small trout, back in his home state of

Curt Gowdy and Stu Apte years later, at a Bonefish & Tarpon Trust Backbone Fishing Tournament, held at the Ocean Reef Club. *Photo by Jeannine Apte.*

Wyoming. He said that his dad taught him how to fish with love and care for the fish and the ecology around him.

The American Sportsman TV show was the longest-running and most-viewed outdoor hunting and fishing show ever. And Curt became known as the American Sportsman. His recognizable voice was not only on the shows he produced, but also heard on *Wide World of Sports,* as the voice of the Red Sox, at Super Bowls, and at many other sporting events.

Everyone who knew Curt could see how much he truly loved to fish and enjoyed the company of skilled anglers in well-known fishing areas like Islamorada in the Florida Keys. During the last couple of years of his life, when his back was hurting so bad, it was difficult for him to spend much time standing in the boat. Still, he went fishing, standing only to cast when a fish was spotted. Anglers would pay a premium for the honor of spending time in the boat with Curt, as he helped promote fund-raising tournaments for conservation causes such as Bonefish and Tarpon Unlimited's Backbone, the Chuck LaMar Pediatric Cancer Research Tournament, the Redbone Celebrity Tournament Series for cystic fibrosis research, and of course, his friend Ted Williams's favorite, the Jimmy Fund.

I first met Curt Gowdy in 1962. He was doing the introduction to an *ABC's Wide World of Sports* show that involved a fly fishing tarpon competition between Al ("AJ") McClane, the angling editor of *Field & Stream* magazine, and Joe Brooks, angling editor of *Outdoor Life* magazine. I was Joe's guide in the show; Jimmie Albright was Al's. The show opened with a very young-looking Curt standing in front of a large banner stretched between two coconut palms, with the old humpback Bahia Honda Bridge in the background.

Forty-two years later, in March 2004, Curt asked me to help do an hour-and-a-half program about the early years of fishing in the Florida Keys at the prestigious Ocean Reef Club in North Key Largo. There was standing room only in the 350-seat theater, typical for any event with Curt on the program.

Without Curt's knowledge, I gave my copy of the 1962 show to the film projectionist. With a prearranged signal at the end of the program, the lights dimmed and on a theater-size screen appeared Curt in front of the *Wide World of Sports* banner as he introduced the show. The audience went wild.

As we walked out of the theater to a room set up with cocktails and hors d'oeuvres, Curt put his arm around my shoulder, giving me a hug. With tears running down his cheeks, he said, "Stu, I didn't even know you had that footage. Thank you so much for bringing it. But, Stu, look what has happened to me."

I smiled at him. "My friend, age has snuck up on us both. That's what is called life."

Two years later, on February 20, 2006, Curt went to that place in heaven where all good American Sportsmen hope to go.

As a footnote, let me add that Curt Gowdy is probably the only person who has been inducted into 20 halls of fame, including broadcasting, sports, conservation, and fishing.

It was my extreme honor to have been inducted into the International Game Fish Association's Fishing Hall of Fame two years after Curt's induction.

chapter 19

Have Tackle, Will Travel

Tips on chasing angling dreams in foreign lands.

Some of my friends on numerous occasions have accused me of overkill when I do things. Maybe it has to do with my navy training as a fighter pilot. Or maybe I'm just naturally tenacious. No matter, but I can tell you the trait sometimes pays off big-time. That's especially true in traveling.

Case in point:

It was 1976, and I was scheduled to cohost an ABC's *American Sportsman* TV show in Costa Rica with Curt Gowdy. Because I was a captain with Pan Am, it was not unusual for me to make our travel arrangements for the whole ABC film crew to fly from Miami to San José, Costa Rica, where we were booked to spend the night before flying in small, single-engine airplanes to the Caribbean coast.

The Shakespeare Company had sent six boxes of spinning reels in various sizes, bait casting reels, and rods for matched setups. Rapala lure company sent a large carton with 15 boxes (six lures in a box) of assorted color combinations of the Countdown 13 swimming plug. (I had previously enjoyed tremendous success with that lure in the area we were going to fish.) The DuPont Company had jumped on board our venture by sending a large carton with thousands of yards of various tests of Stren monofilament line.

When we arrived in San José after our 2½ hour nonstop flight from Miami, all our luggage got there except . . . *arggrh!* . . . the containers of lures and reels. After the

Pan Am people did some extensive checking, we learned the package had gone onto a flight to Rio de Janeiro, Brazil, that had been leaving about the same time we did.

This is when the Stu Apte cautionary preparations kicked in. I had a carry-on bag with enough spinning reels, bait-casting reels, and lures to carry us through the first three days of a seven-day filming trip.

Now let's fast-forward to the present.

Since the terrorist attack on 9/11, gone are the "good old days" when you could carry a tackle box full of flies/lures/hooks and even a mini Swiss Army knife on the airplane with you to make sure they arrive at the destination when you do. I will have to admit that when you ship them with your luggage, they do make it around 85 percent of the time. What do you do the other 15 percent if your fishing destination is somewhere in Africa, up the Rupununi River in Guyana or any other great fishing destination off the beaten path?

Mostly, you wait and hope. Carry-on restrictions are so tight, and vary with airlines to the point where you have to check them in advance, that some of my former tactics may not work. Such as carrying on rod cases and a couple of reels in my carry-on bag. You may try, but they may end up with your checked luggage.

One reason four-piece rods have become so popular today is because the rod case fits easily into your checked baggage.

On a sailfish trip, my billfish flies are attached to made-up leaders, with size 5/0 or 6/0 hooks, and are packed in my suitcase and hopefully travel in the belly to my destination. But, I will carry at least a dozen billfish tube flies without any hooks in my carry-on bag. That way, if push came to shove and my luggage is lost or delayed en route, I could beg, borrow, or steal hooks and leader material.

I pack one pair of polarized glasses and an extra pair of regular glasses and carry one pair of each in my carry-on bag. I always carry my camera case on the airplane. For trips abroad, it's very important always to have two extra photocopies of your passport, one in your suitcase being shipped and one on your person.

My next "must have" item comes from the School of Hard Knocks. Having learned the following lesson, I always pack a light rain suit with my clothing.

I had been carrying rain gear all these many years without ever having to put it on. That was until my trip for the Third Annual Stu Apte Fly Fishing Sailfish Tournament in Costa Rica. We had an equatorial front push north and go stationary over us for four days—and, yes, you guessed it, that was the only time I did not take a rain suit with me on a trip. I came in from fishing each day looking like a wet rag.

Remember, you may have to vary your specialized clothing and fishing tackle, depending the climate and the type of fishing you'll be doing. Hot, cold; wet, dry; wading, boat riding? Sometimes you'll be headed for a destination where all of the above are possible. You can start loading up weight totals real fast, especially when you add in waders. On top of all that, you need dry comfortable clothes and shoes for relaxing in the lodge. It all mounts up, and it can be damn expensive with today's baggage "extra" costs or going overweight.

Many golfers ship their clubs to their destinations. Many anglers might want to follow suit when they have a lot of heavy stuff.

Boat rides to and from the fishing spots at your destination must be considered, or you're heading for misery. From bonefishing to fishing Alaska's salmon and trout rivers, and many places in between, you'll be spending some time in boats, whether you fish from them or not. You'll need wet gear to keep you from spray and wind, hats that will stay on your head (or a hood) and eye protection to boot. You'll also need a "wet bag," where you stow your camera and personal items. Whether it's raining or not, most boat rides are wet to some extent.

There are some items I would feel lost without, so if my wife is going with me on the trip, as she generally does, I will put one of the following items in each of our suitcases, increasing the odds that at least one of them will make it to our destination.

1. My mini Swiss Army Knife. (I use the scissors for trimming leaders.)
2. Lipstick-moisturizer with SPF 45 protection.
3. Ocean Potion oil-free sunblock, with SPF 50, UVA1, UVA2, and UVB protection.
4. Extra rigged fly lines and a bobbin with Kevlar thread. Sometimes the security in some countries (Canada and Costa Rica, to name two) will not let you carry fly lines on your reel on board the airplane.
5. Camera battery charger, and electric converter if necessary. Sun gloves, and a cap with up-downer bill and flap for ear and neck sun protection, SunClava for sun and wind protection, Neosporin antibiotic, waterproof Band-Aids, ibuprofen, and Extra-Strength Tylenol for those long hard fights with trophy fish or to help with having to sleep on a soft mattress.
6. If you are interested in setting a world record on your trip, you should carry an IGFA-certified Boga-Grip. They come in 15-pound, 30-pound, and 60-pound sizes. Depending on the size of the fish you might be catching, you can purchase it and have it certified by IGFA.

Before every trip to new, far places, it's imperative that you do some thorough research on items you might not be able to purchase there. You might be surprised at what you learn.

I have fished every continent except Antarctica during the past 60 years, and these tips are the best advice I can send your way about coping with travel issues. Be aware that security and baggage restrictions are tight, vary among airlines, and must be checked out when planning your trip. Nothing I can tell you here will cover all situations.

As an example of how crazy some airline things are, consider that you'll have to give up your tiny penknife at the security check-in. But if you're traveling first class, on some airlines they may even give you a steak knife to cut your meat.

Go figure!

chapter 20

Today's Menu Special: Shrimp!

When fish are hungry, serve them this incredible edible treat.

Of all the many live baits that can be used for inshore fishing, the incredible and edible shrimp is without a doubt the most popular. Why not? Fish love shrimp, and you can eat your leftover bait. That's a win–win situation.

There are many ways of using shrimp as bait for the large variety of fish that enjoy having a shrimp snack, as we humans often do. (See my wife's recipe for coconut fried shrimp at the end of this article.) I'm going to share with you the go-to tactics I've developed for using shrimp during my years of guiding and angling, to great success.

For this old backcountry guide, bonefish come first to mind when we're talking shrimp.

Thirty or 40 years ago, I thought it was imperative to use the Wright & McGill Eagle Claw 189, size 1/0 or 2/0 hooks, because of the bait-holding barbs on the hook shanks. These hooks have an offset bend that I would straighten with my pliers. Nowadays, I generally use 2/0 or occasionally 3/0 Owner Aki hooks, depending on the size of the shrimp. They are super sharp with a very small barb, making it much easier to release the bonefish.

I'll show you my two main ways of using live shrimp, not just for bonefish but for any number of seafood specials.

Facing. Flip Pallot just tailed Stu's 38-pound permit, an IGFA world record on 6-pound-class line.

First and foremost, twist off the tail. (Back in my guiding days, I sometimes bit it off, just for the fun of seeing my clients' reaction.) From underneath, insert the point of the hook where the tail had been and thread the shrimp onto the hook so that the point barely protrudes from its belly, having the shrimp lie almost straight out on the hook.

The reason for this is threefold: (1) Without the tail acting as an airfoil, creating wind resistance, the shrimp casts easier and more accurately. (2) With the tail removed, the shrimp acts as natural chum, giving off important scent. (3) Having the shrimp without its tail almost straight on the hook, you can retrieve it backwards without it spinning. That backward motion is the natural movement a shrimp makes when it is startled by one of its many predators.

The other way I sometimes hook a large (4 or 5 inches long) live shrimp is to fish it as a swimming shrimp. I insert the hook from underneath through its head, being careful not to penetrate the black organ, which would kill it. Make your cast in front of and beyond the fish you are casting to, start a very slow retrieve that makes the shrimp swim along naturally.

Even when it's tough getting tarpon or snook to eat a lure, they will seldom refuse a well-presented shrimp hooked this way.

Almost as important as preparing your shrimp on the hook is your presentation. For shallow-water tailing bonefish, cast in front of and beyond the fish in the direction it is feeding. Just as your shrimp reaches the water, put your pointing finger toward the spool, stopping the line from coming off the reel while slowly raising the rod tip at the same time. That makes the bait slide as it softly hits the water, creating the illusion of a shrimp skipping on the surface to get away.

When finding bonefish in 2 feet or water (more if it's windy), I'll sometimes use a split shot attached to my leader or double line right next to the hook's eye to expedite my bait's reaching the bottom. In calm conditions, be aware you'll not be able to cast so close to the fish as you can in windy, riled conditions.

Last year while fishing the Redbone Tournament in Islamorada, I found myself in adverse weather conditions, needing only a bonefish to be in the winner's circle. My fishing partner and I had already caught quite a number of redfish in the Flamingo area, and with 2½ hours of fishing left before quitting time, we decided to see if we could conjure up a bonefish or two in the Buchanan Keys area. It was both overcast and windy, but my good friend Capt. Dave Denkert, our guide, knew a particular spot the bonefish passed through on this phase of the outgoing tide. (Location! Location! Location!)

Captain Dave shoved his pushpole into the soft bottom and tied onto it while I broke out a couple of my ace-in-the-hole hooks—Gamakatsu G-Lock 2/0 hooks normally used for plastic baits. Quickly tying one onto my line and partner Mike Pehanich's as well, I put a split shot near the hook's eye and broke one shrimp in half,

How Stu hooks up silver dollar-sized finny crabs, probably the best of all permit bait.

The deep silver sides of a permit reflect its surroundings and making it almost invisible at times. Anglers and guides look for the black tail and black tip of the dorsal fin.

threading it onto the hook, then twisted the tails off two other shrimp, threading them onto this long-shank hook to face in opposite directions. That was a little trick I had learned from another dear friend, Capt. Rick Murphy. Sometimes it works.

Mike was sitting behind me and on the side of the boat, so we cast our baits in different directions. I placed my spinning rod in a rod holder alongside the con-

sole and kind of hunkered back, thinking pleasant thoughts. After about 15 minutes, we both had hook-ups at almost the same moment. My fish took off on the type of run a small bonefish might make. It appeared as though Mike's was doing the same thing. Wow, a doubleheader. What a bonus that would be for us.

O shades of gloom and dark despair, both our fish turned out to be bonnethead sharks. Oh well, sometimes that's the price you pay when dunking shrimp for bonefish.

Dave once again baited both our rigs and we cast them back into the same area. After sticking my rod back into the rod holder, I once again kicked back. Keeping half an eye on my line, I may actually have dropped off into a little nap. Suddenly, my line bounced a couple of times. That got my full attention. When I pulled the rod from the holder, I noticed that I had a lot of slack line. Rapidly winding the slack in while dropping my rod tip toward the water, I continued reeling in until I felt resistance. I set the hook with two sharp jabs.

This critter took off like one hell of a big bonefish, and it looked like I was going to be stripped of all my line. Captain Dave had the pushpole out of the mud and was feverishly poling downwind after my big "bonefish." I breathed easier when the creature stopped before all my line melted. Now I was able to work this fish by pumping and winding as Captain Dave moved me toward it.

Ten minutes later, we were close enough to be disappointed with what we saw. A big permit had found and picked up my shrimp cluster off the bottom. All I needed to be Grand Celebrity Champion of the Redbone Tournament was a bonefish that measured at least 19 inches, and what did I catch? A permit that weighed considerably more than 19 pounds. I guess you would call that a good luck, bad luck story. I think it shows you a lot about the mixed bag opportunities of fishing shrimp.

All the techniques for rigging shrimp mentioned above can be used for redfish, saltwater trout, and even striped bass. If you like casting ⅛- to ⅜-ounce jigs, a surefire way of producing more strikes is to "tip your jig" with a small piece of shrimp. Don't use too large a piece of shrimp, and don't hook it from underneath. If you hook it from the back, the piece of shrimp will swim with the lure instead of spinning, having a more natural action.

Oh, that incredible edible shrimp.

JEANNINE APTE'S COCONUT-FRIED SHRIMP

My wife shares our favorite shrimp recipe.

1   cup milk
2   large eggs
1   teaspoon salt
½   teaspoon coarse black pepper
1   packet Oven Fry (Extra Crispy Pork—"It's like Shake 'N Bake—only better!")
½   cup finely shredded coconut
    vegetable oil (enough to cover the shrimp in a large skillet)
1   pound fresh shrimp

In a large bowl, beat the milk and eggs.
Add the salt and pepper, mix well, and set aside.

Lay out approximately 12 inches of waxed paper on the counter, and
spread the contents of the Oven Fry packet onto one side of it.
Spread the shredded coconut on the other half of the waxed paper.

Dip the shrimp into the egg mixture to moisten, and then shake off
the excess liquid. Lightly press the moistened shrimp onto the coconut,
coating all sides; repeat the process with the Oven Fry.

Heat the oil in a large skillet, and add the battered shrimp.
Fry the shrimp for approximately 10 minutes, adjusting cooking time
relative to the size of the shrimp. Turn frequently in order to keep the
coconut from burning and serve immediately.

Serves 4

Facing. How Stu hooks up a shrimp for the swimming
shrimp bait, being careful not to penetrate the black organ,
killing the shrimp and making it far less effective.

Stu and Carl Yastrzemski (Yaz) at the New England Sportsmen Show.

Jazzing It with Yaz

Ted Williams wasn't the only member of the Boston Red
Sox with fishing prowess. Here's how Carl Yastrzemski
brought down the house in a clinic we did together.

The time was November 1961. My soon-to-be wife and I were spending the first of many Thanksgiving dinners with Ted Williams at his new home in Islamorada in the Florida Keys. His former home, a ground-level structure on the ocean side of Islamorada, was gutted and almost completely destroyed on September 9 the previous year by Hurricane Donna.

Ted had a new bride of two months named Lee Howard, and while she was preparing a fantastic turkey dinner with all the trimmings, Ted was telling me about a new left fielder the Boston Red Sox had signed.

"Stu, you won't be able to pronounce his name, but you will damn sure remember it. Carl Yastrzemski will no doubt be a good replacement for Teddy Ballgame."

For sure, Ted knew what he was talking about. Yaz, as he was affectionately called, became a solid player his first two years and then emerged as a rising star in 1963, winning the American League batting championship with a batting average of .321 and leading the league in doubles and walks. He enjoyed his best season in 1967 by capturing the American League Triple Crown with a .326 batting average, 44 home runs, and 121 RBIs. He was the last hitter to win the Triple Crown and was voted the American League's Most Valuable Player almost unanimously.

In 1969, Yaz hit the first of two consecutive 40 home run seasons as he led the Red Sox to third-place finishes. Yaz got four hits and won the All-Star Game MVP Award in 1970, even though the American League lost. His .329 batting average that season was his career high.

For the past three years, I had been working as a fishing consultant for the Du-Pont Company, helping develop and promote its new Stren Monofilament Fishing Line. Part of my job was performing at various sportsmen shows around the country, which included the New England Sportsmen's Show. There, I was doing three 40-minute casting demonstrations on center stage in front of approximate 12,000 people. Whenever possible, I would team up with a local hero onstage and then spend time as a guest answering questions and signing autographs in booths.

My first such performance was with Ken Harrelson (aka "the Hawk"), who wanted to learn how to be a better fly fisherman. Building upon his great timing and coordination, it was an easy job for me, and in no time at all he was casting twice the distance he previously could.

My next performance was on center stage with Carl Yastrzemski and brought a standing-room-only crowd of more than 12,000 because of the promotion on radio, TV, in newspapers, and large billboards throughout the War Memorial Coliseum. This time, I would instruct Yaz on the best way to cast for accuracy and distance with an open-face Ted Williams 400 Spinning Reel.

Using a ¼-ounce rubber skish lure made for practice casting, he was casting it with bull's-eye accuracy right off the bat—pun intended. He picked it up so fast that in order for me to be onstage the prescribed 40 minutes, I had to come up with some trick ways of casting to teach him, like the bow-and-arrow cast and stepping-on-the-lure cast for extremely confined areas. Yaz was a quick study on each of the different ways to cast, making it difficult for me to stretch the time onstage. The audience would go wild after each demonstration, and it was obvious that Yaz was really enjoying the program.

Then it happened. When I bent over to pick up an ultralight spinning outfit for a slightly different demonstration, the black Sharpie permanent marker in the top pocket of my shirt fell at my feet. I had been using it to autograph caps while spending time between shows in various booths.

It came to me like a bolt out of the blue: A unique way to close this performance would be having Carl Yastrzemski sign *Yaz* on the small ⅛-ounce skish lure attached to the ultralight, 2-pound-test spinning outfit, and dangle it in front of him with the bail open and have him knock it into the upper tier for a "home run."

We were wearing small wireless microphones, so the entire audience heard me ask Yaz if he would autograph and hit the little lure into the upper deck. I just needed to get someone to run a baseball bat up to the stage. The audience started a deafening chant of *"Yaz—Yaz—Yaz!"* that was the most unbelievable thing I had ever heard.

This was no sooner said than a Louisville Slugger from a nearby booth was passed up to me. After handing it to Yaz, I quickly stepped back, giving him room to take a few practice swings the way he would before stepping up to the plate. Quickly I explained to him how I would be out of the way while dangling the small lure, with the line resting on my forefinger, bail open as though I were going to cast. I figured that when the bat made contact, one of two things would happen: The lure would fly, streaming fishing line behind it, or the shock would be so great that the 2-pound-test line would break as the lure flew into the upper deck.

Yaz stepped into position, tapping the bat on the stage as though it were home plate. The audience fell quiet.

Taking a deep breath and holding it to make sure I did not move the lure, I waited.

There was a *swish* but no *splat* as Yaz had a swing and a miss. The audience

Stu Apte showing Yaz the skish lure he was going to have Yaz sign before hitting it into the upper tiers of expo hall.

went wild with cheers. Yaz turned to me, forgetting he had a microphone on, and said, "Stu, why did you move it?"

"Honest, Yaz," I answered. "I didn't move anything. Remember, it's only an inch and a half long, and you're used to hitting something a lot bigger."

The audience started the *"Yaz!"* chant again as I stepped back, again dangling the small lure. This time he connected with a home run, knocking it into the very top row.

We could not repeat that performance, despite all the cheers that greeted it. Hitting the lure into the audience carried the potential of injuring someone.

For all who were there that day, Yaz's "home run" at the New England Sportsmen's Show was one of his most memorable ever.

An underwater view makes it easy to see how the cobia can be mistaken for a shark. *Photo by Pat Ford.*

Cobia: The Shark Impostor

At first sight, you're thinking "Shark!" Then, "Amberjack?" Then, as the line melts from your reel, the cobia lets you know who's boss.

A rose by any other name may still be a rose, but a South Atlantic and U.S. Gulf Coast fish by any other name is likely to be a cobia.

Depending upon where you happen to be fishing, from the Carolina's south to Georgia and Florida, then up the Gulf Coast to Louisiana and over to Texas, that sharklike brown shape you see barreling down on your just-hooked seatrout, live blue runner, or crab bait might be called any number of descriptive names the locals have for it. These include lemonfish, ling, brown bomber, and crabeater.

But it's really an offbeat impostor wearing a shark suit as a disguise. It's the cobia, a fish that has earned the reputation for a different kind of fight, strange habits, intelligence of sorts, and fine eating, when properly prepared.

The cobia isn't even remotely related to the shark. It doesn't have teeth, but a soft lip and a serrated mouth, like another south coast favorite, the tarpon. But it's not even a cousin of old silversides, or the amberjacks that often hang around the same wrecks and shallow Gulf reefs, feeding on the same tidbits. In fact, this brown-backed, light-bellied impostor is in a class by itself—its own species—a rare item in today's world, an individual.

Its feeding preferences vary from the norm, and this predilection sometimes misleads anglers to think of sharks. Cobias primarily prefer crustaceans, shrimps, crabs, and crawfish, but will also feast on almost any kind of live fish they can grab. Most first-timers encounter cobias when they just hooked a fat seatrout, or have a snapper,

Often confused with a shark at first sight, the cobia is an exciting game fish that will test your skills and tackle. *Photo by Pat Ford.*

grunt, or blue runner on their line. Out of nowhere zooms the cobia, wearing its shark disguise, and inhales the hapless fish. Scratch one table star, but chalk up another.

In late spring and early summer, cobias start an annual migration back up from the Caribbean. As these schools approach the Florida Keys, they begin to part company; some venture out into the Atlantic Ocean following the coast up to Georgia and the Carolinas. Others meander along the Gulf Coast of Florida on their way to Mobile Bay, Biloxi, New Orleans, and points west, where by the midsummer months of July and August, the whole Gulf Coast down to Brownsville, Texas, offers the lemonfish as a specialty.

Drop your bait over a wreck, alongside an oil rig, bridge piling, or channel marker, and you'll likely come up with a prize that has been lurking down there, feasting on the smaller fish and crustaceans that inhabit the protected areas. In early morning, particularly before the boat traffic starts, you can often slip up on resident cobias around river buoys, bridge pilings, or even a single channel marker. Turn your engine off a respectable distance out, setting up a drift. You might see a number of cobias lying on the surface like sunbathers or casually milling around just underneath. You'll find that they seem to have little fear, continuing their circling if not disturbed.

One way to get their interest is by hanging a chum sack in the water and dropping a few ladles of chum over the side. Then hook a lively blue runner just ahead of the dorsal fin, using a 6/0 short-shank hook, about 8 feet of 50-pound-test monofilament, and a fairly long, stout rod. Ring their dinner bell by swishing this setup in figure eights at the surface, and you'll soon be looking down at some hungry cobias.

Normally, it won't be long before you hook up with one of the brown bombers. Quite a number of artificial lures will work as well—once the fish get into the feeding mode. Blue runners are a favorite live bait, but you can also use pinfish, shrimps, squids, eels, or crabs.

There are some places in Florida Bay and Tampa Bay where I particularly enjoy fishing for cobias. With a light breeze and reasonably good visibility, I will drift into those areas, holding a 10-weight fly rod rigged with a 5-inch-long eel fly attached to 12 inches of 40-pound-test mono as my bite tippet.

If I don't see any cobias when I drift past —and providing I don't have any teasing gear on board—I will try appealing to the fish's curious nature. After starting my engine and making two complete circles around the area, I'll shut down and wait. I'll watch for their brown backs, then offer them my eel-like fly.

In the Keys and Florida Bay, the very finest bait for cobias is a sandperch. Probably the second best is the lizardfish, which somewhat resembles the sandperch. Both species are bottom feeders, and the cobias seem to regard them as special table fare. Also, in the past couple of years, I have personally had great success using the artificial eel.

Most anglers fishing the shallow wrecks and channel markers use heavy-duty spinning tackle or hefty conventional gear with a star-drag reel to prevent the cobia from charging back into the metal jungle, or around the barnacle-crusted marker, and cutting them off. With either class of tackle, I highly recommend using the fairly new, superstrong, abrasion-resistant, tight-braid lines. My personal preference of the last few years is a tight braid produced by Sufix (Rapala).

Another strange part of this fish's personality is its curiosity. I remember coming upon a whole herd of cobias just off of Key Largo, where they were lying on the surface enjoying the sun, lollygagging like a barnyard full of hogs. When we came too close with the boat, they would dive, only to bob back to the surface as soon as we were far enough away to be nonthreatening. We did manage to circle back upwind, setting up a drift, and we had a doubleheader hookup using live pinfish, with their dorsal fins trimmed off. In that instance, trolling would have dispersed the cobias, either sending them on their way or putting them down to the bottom.

A great way to fish for cobias along Florida's northern Gulf of Mexico and the South Atlantic coast of North Florida and Georgia is to watch for large mantas or leopard whiprays offshore. One of those rays is liable to have half a dozen large cobias swimming alongside it in excellent fighter-plane formation.

Look for one of the rays to jump sometimes, or you might just catch the flick of its wingtip as it breaks the surface. Position the boat ahead of it, shut down the engine, and cast your bait to them as they swim past. If the cobias that happen to be swimming alongside are still undisturbed, you will no doubt be hooked up with a superb fighting and eating fish upwards of 30 pounds.

Cobia is excellent to eat when properly prepared. Fillet and skin them, making sure to remove every last bit of red, dark meat—the gamy stuff. What's left is white, flaky, and delicious.

Cut the fillets into finger-size chunks and fry them; slab the meat into steaks and broil; or bake the whole fillet. Cobia is nothing less than delicious, no matter how you cook it.

Just last week, I made some fantastic ceviche by dicing the fillet into thumbnail-size chunks, mixed with diced onions and marinated in key lime juice and vinegar, seasoned with salt and black pepper. I added bits of jalapeño pepper, also cut to thumbnail size, making it easy to find and remove. Marinating takes around 2 to 3 hours, and when the flesh turns an opaque white, you and your friends are in for a mouthwatering treat.

Tailing an Atlantic salmon in Iceland, Stu gets off to a great start,
with rain clouds threatening and the light perfect for fishing.

chapter 23

Viking Salmon

*Iceland's volcanic landscape, once the sanctuary of the
Vikings, is crisscrossed with bright rivers filled with bright
salmon. For the fly fisher, opportunity abounds.*

In a quiet pool the size of a football field, between the waterfall and where I stand in my hip waders stripping line from my fly reel, the air-clear water teems with masses of Atlantic salmon. It seems like a whole world of them. They jam into the pool, stacked like so many shimmering cords of wood, each waiting its turn at the rapids. The fish the Romans named Salar, "the Leaper."

Single salmon move restlessly, milling around, joining into ever-tightening schools, intermittently leaping into the air so that at times a half dozen fish are airborne. I absentmindedly reach up to adjust my polarized glasses, as though they are playing tricks on my vision. I have not expected to see so many Atlantic salmon in all of Iceland. My fishing partner, Jim Chapralis, agrees.

At one time or another, we had fished the salmon rivers of Norway, Ireland, and Labrador. On those trips, it seemed that the waters were too high or too low, too muddy or too clear, or too seldom filled with fish. Now, the Laxá í Kjós, this swift, transparent ribbon only an hour's drive from bustling Reykjavík, holds the promise of being a salmon fisherman's ultimate utopia.

"I'm going to try a dry fly," I announce.

Jim grins. "Go ahead and be stubborn about it, but you've been warned."

Stu's Hardy Princess fly reel, with some favorite Atlantic
salmon flies displayed on the salmon's side.

True, I had been told that salmon just won't take a dry fly in this river, but it's the way I prefer to fish, and I am determined. I quickly strip off a length of line, tie on the size 10 White Wulff, and shoot out a long cast. At the same time, Jim drops a blue Hairy Mary wet fly into a group of two dozen fish and begins working it slowly across the current. Nothing happens.

The fish ignore both of us. Twenty minutes go by as we cast to them, teasing, coaxing, and courting them. Sometimes a fish leaps, playfully it seems, over our lines, leaders, and flies, but there are no takers.

"I've got one," Jim says. Then just as quickly, "Nope, he's off."

Finally, at the end of a drift, a salmon rises to my fly. The hook pulls out almost immediately, but contrary to what I have been advised, it takes my dry fly. I change tactics slightly, trying to provoke more action. I slip a Portland Creek hitch on a size 8 Blue Charm, which is simply a half hitch wrapped around the body about one third of the way back from the hook's eye. This method (also called "the Riffling hitch") was developed in Eastern Canada and is quite simple, and often deadly. The fly skates across the surface, leaving a V-wake. I hold my rod tip up and strip in slowly. It was more than one fish could resist.

The water dimpled under my fly and I feel the strong pull that spells "salmon." My trout rod doubles over, and the reel shrieks as line zips off the spool. The fish jumps four times, thrashing toward the waterfall before its strength starts to go. It turns downstream and jumps again, my reel screaming as though its gears are burning up. Just as suddenly as the mad dash begins, it ends. The salmon has reached a deeper pool, giving it a false feeling of security.

Reeling furiously, I work my way downstream toward this Viking spirit. The wild leaps and hard fighting runs are just too much for my adversary. From my newly acquired position, I pump and reel until finally the fish scraps across the gravelly bank and I haul it out by the tail—10 pounds of beautiful Atlantic salmon. It is the first in a number of adventurous encounters on a dream-fishing trip with some of the hardest-fighting salmon in the world.

This trip to Iceland, like so many of the best fishing trips I've been on, was conceived under unusual circumstances halfway around the world in Nepal. A mutual acquaintance of Jim Chapralis and mine is Jim Edwards, managing director of Tiger Tops, an unusual lodge in Nepal's Himalayas. Edwards, a British subject who married a lovely Icelandic girl, brings his family home to Iceland for the cool summers.

The last time I spoke with him, Jim told me about the fantastic salmon fishing in Iceland's rivers, *laxás* as they are called there. He insisted that Jim Chapralis and I visit them in the summer. Believe me, he didn't have to ask twice. We scheduled the trip for midsummer, July 10 to 19, in three separate locations.

Approaching the coast of this strange island of dazzling ice and black lava, I look down at the pale sea. The wakes of fishing boats point their Vs away from land, moving out of a wall of ghostly fog. Cod, haddock, and herring boats are following the strong tradition of Iceland's men of the sea.

Norsemen from Scandinavia and Celts from Ireland settled Iceland, and the resultant mixture was successful in many ways. The women are among the most beautiful on earth. Of all the Nordic peoples, Icelanders alone produced great literature in the Middle Ages. The birth rate is the highest in Europe, and the death rate one of the lowest in the world—7 per 1,000 annually. Though there are 200,000 people in an area of the size of Kentucky, most live in 14 towns and 40 villages on the coast.

Since we are not scheduled to fish until the next day, Jim and I rent a Volkswagen to drive the 50 miles from Reykjavík to our lodge on the Laxá í Kjós.

Rolling through the barren countryside, it was easy to see why the American astronauts trained in this part of Iceland for their moon landing. It's a harsh land, where wood is so scarce, a property buyer pays for all driftwood rights as we do for mineral rights here in the United States. The sprawling Vatnajökull glacier is larger than all the glaciers in Europe combined. There are 700 thermal springs; our word "geyser" comes from Iceland's Great Geysir, which spews up a 180-foot column of hot water. There are 30 active volcanoes, including Askja, which had its latest eruption in 1961, and Surtsey, which came boiling out of the flat sea belching fire and steam in 1963.

All this activity makes for interesting weather patterns, and you can experience almost any kind on any given day. Temperatures, though, average a mild 31 degrees

The late Gene Hill, columnist and author, was all smiles
when he displayed this Icelandic salmon.

Fahrenheit in January and a San Francisco–like 52 degrees in summer. Warm winds
from the Gulf Stream hold off the Arctic blasts.

Far off in the distance, the snow still drapes the mountain tops, and moist air
blowing in from the sea brings a wall of thick fog over us without a moment's notice.
In two miles, it is clear again. The road meanders through the flat meadows with
sheep and horses grazing, and over streams where geese paddled.

After our first success, we have numerous hook-ups as our luck seems to change.
Jim moves to the other side of the river and strikes a fine strong salmon that has him
climbing goatlike over the rocks as the fish heads downstream. He is using a very
light split-bamboo fly rod and a light tippet that doesn't allow for any horsing around.
I watch as his fish jumps, runs, then jumps again while Jim clambers after it, giving
line, cranking stubbornly, pumping. Eventually, 200 yards downstream, Jim ends
the drama splendidly, tailing a fine 9½-pound Atlantic salmon.

We find that long casts are not necessary, and more than once I labor the point, extending only a few feet of fly line beyond the rod tip. With one fish, I drop the fly right
at the foot of the waterfall and let the current bounce it out of the surface. A salmon
takes it on the splash and the fight is wild before I tail a 13-pounder. This area at the

falls is thick with salmon preparing for their amazing leaps upstream to spawn. Reportedly, Atlantic salmon refuse to eat during their spawning run, but at different times each day, they strike anyway, for whatever mysterious reason, and it is possible to hook as many as two or three fish on a single retrieve.

These Icelandic salmon are not of great size, but they fight like heavyweights. One fish rolls right out of the water at my dry fly, but misses it. It repeats this maneuver three times, and I am sure I'll get it. Broad shouldered, it looks as if it will easily go 25 to 30 pounds. On such great salmon rivers as Quebec's Moisie or Norway's Alta, this fish would hardly grab rave notices. But in Iceland, where the average salmon might run 8 to 12 pounds, fish of this size are considered not only outstanding, but rare as well.

Iceland has about 60 salmon rivers that rate among the best anywhere, and Icelanders are quick to explain that their salmon do not migrate to the Greenland salmon rendezvous area where the Danes, especially, have each year been

A couple of Atlantic salmon from the cold, beautiful waters of Iceland, along with the types of flies used.

hauling out thousands of tons of migrating salmon from the British Isles and Eastern Canada. Many other countries have permitted their commercial fisheries to heavily net their own waters. Norway was a good example, as were most Canadian provinces.

Commercial netting has been all but abolished in Iceland, and the government has enforced regulations that allow only a 90-day season for sport fishing. Which is not permitted between 1 P.M. and 4 P.M., relieving the rivers of heavy angling pressure.

The next day, Jim and I stand with our guide, Stephan, just below another waterfall and watch dozens of salmon congregate at a sharp bend.

"Crouch low on that big rock," Stephan warns me. "They may not scare away, but for sure they won't take if they see you."

Lying practically on my belly, with the fly tied to a 6-pound-test tapered leader; I am using an 8-weight fly rod, the same one that I have used many times in the Florida Keys for bonefish.

Stu's gillie is showing off a tough-fighting Atlantic salmon from an Icelandic river.

Though I can see that Stephan has chosen his favorite Nighthawk fly from my box, I have picked out the Muddler Minnow, a trout fly. I crouch low, my eyes barely peeking over the huge rock, and begin flicking the fly into a small area of the bend. Sometimes I let the fly drift au naturel to the fish; other times I give it a little action. They refuse to take, though a couple of times I do move some fish.

Jim is having the same problems. "Uncatchable," I hear him mutter.

I am about to agree. Just a few more casts, I figure, maybe five minutes more. Okay, three minutes, and then back to the lodge for lunch. We'll be late once again. I can't help but see a big one show with a slow, deliberate roll. I want to hit him, hit him fast like you sometimes do when brown trout fishing. But with salmon, you wait until the fish turns. I tighten up the line with my left hand while raising the rod with my right, setting the hook.

With a start, I suddenly become aware of this fish's probable escape route: first downstream, then down the chute into the canyon. You have to anticipate where a fish will go before he does it, especially in a treacherous area like this. The salmon circles the pool twice, then flashes out into the fast current. I leap up and run after him, trying to head him off. Then I have to cross the river, which oozes cold water over the tops of my hip waders. I scramble over the rocks, thankful for the felt soles on my waders, lifting my line away from the crevices and tightening up again, pressuring the fish, coaxing him away from places that might chafe my light tippet. Then he gives out. I ease him into a backwater behind a large boulder. Suddenly, it seems, he is at my feet and I am lifting him out by the tail, a hefty 15½-pounder. This is one day I don't mind being late for lunch.

It is here I see another phenomenon that supports one of my pet theories. Standing over the largest pool of the *laxá* in late afternoon just as the tide comes in, I observe a huge concentration of salmon gathering at the river mouth. Each time the same peak conditions occur—floodtide and late afternoon on the full or new moon—it happens. There is a big push of fish invariably moving into the river from the ocean. I have observed this hundreds of times with my favorite game fish, tarpon, and am not too surprised Atlantic salmon follow the same pattern. The lower pools of Laxá í Kjós were jammed with a thousand fish. By morning, there are only 100 or so left after the masses have made their way upriver during the night.

When our three days of fishing are over, I have landed 24 salmon, Jim has taken 13, and between us, we have hooked well over 100. You might ask why so many got away. Well, the honest fact is simply that Jim and I decided not to use a net, tailer, or gaff, and to handle all our own fish. Of course, our gillie thought we were out of our minds. "Gillie" is a European name for a guide whose responsibilities include taking care of the river.

Icelandic fishing, like practically any good Atlantic salmon fishing, is quite expensive. In the early 1970s, a visitor could count on at least $150 a day to fish the superb rivers like Laxá í Kjós. Today, prices have risen to astronomical levels.

All too soon, it is time for us to leave. I can't help thinking that Leif Erikson sailed from here in a Viking ship 500 years before Columbus and landed on the American continent. I know life must have been harder then, but I wonder if he was as anxious to return to Iceland as I am.

1,000-pound black marlin roam the Great Barrier Reef off Australia.

2,000-Pound Acrobat—With a Sword!

They call them "granders" along Australia's Great Barrier Reef. Black marlin over 1,000 pounds. And somewhere out there is the "grandest" of them all—a 2,000-pounder.

Half a world away, the land Down Under is a menagerie of great differences, of weird and wonderful animals, of a barrier reef that stands 50 miles offshore and runs 1,200 miles, and unusual species of fish with strange-sounding names.

To the average American angler, "lunkers" mean bass that weigh 10 pounds or tarpon of 100 pounds. But at the Great Barrier Reef of Australia, the biggest of the entire world's game fish dwarf those species into insignificance. The South Pacific's giant black marlin tips the scales at more than 1,000 pounds. Fishing for them is a once-in-a-lifetime thrill, and the first sighting is a never-to-be-forgotten experience.

Come along, and you'll see what I'm talking about.

The spear breaks water first, waving menacingly over the bait, and the awed senses of a stateside angler are mocked by the size of the thing. It is not the slender, graceful rapier of the sailfish that every saltwater fisherman covets to decorate his mantel-piece. It is the thick, blunt, baseball-bat-size cudgel of glowing ultramarine blue, driven by an underwater torpedo the size and speed of a ski boat. It is a giant black marlin. A grander black marlin—a fish weighing at least 1,000 pounds—is incredible, a neon-flashing, dark blue game fish.

Angler JoJo Del Guercio is hooked up to a black
Marlin that turned out to be a 1,000-pounder.

The bill rises up, and a frantic 2-pound baitfish is swallowed like a tadpole to a 20-pound bass. The angler counts four, five, six, up to ten seconds during his free-spool drop back, then hears his captain shout, "Lock up!" He throws the clutch on his huge Fin-Nor reel to its striking position and braces himself to absorb the crunching pull of the 45-pound drag. He winds as fast as his arm will turn as his captain bolts the diesel engines forward to set the hook. In the sudden surge, the giant is tethered, struggling at the long end of the 130-pound-class line. The ultimate trophy, the grander, is only as far away as the angler's stamina and skill will allow it to be. From then on, it's a matter between fisherman and fish.

This year, the Australian capital of marlin fishing, Cairns, weighed in its 100th giant of over 1,000 pounds. The all-tackle record is 1,560 pounds, but even that figure is not the mark modern anglers seek. Instead it's the big one-ton black marlin—the 2,000-pounder that professionals are certain lurks somewhere off the Great Barrier Reef.

For the dedicated fisherman who lands it, the 2,000-pound black marlin will be worth the risks to life and equipment it will take, the tremendous expense, and the time it takes to gain the expertise and to fight the many battles. To the men and women who seek the legend, those are merely conditions of the quest. The prospect of taking the behemoth, which is as agile in its own element as a brook trout is in a rushing stream, is the grandest challenge of all, even if it is the most expensive.

One of those men is Mike Levitt, of Gladwyne, Pennsylvania, who is my host this November in 1976 for 14 days of marlin hunting off Cairns, Australia. Also among the guests are Mike's brother, Skip Levitt, and Ron Jones, who skippers Mike's *Jersey Devil* in the Atlantic. Our fishing takes place from the charter boat *Yanu III*, captained by Paul Whelan, with crewmen Rick Thislewait (the wireman) and Lance Knight (the gaff man). At the end of each fishing day, our accommodations are aboard an 85-foot mother ship *Ulysses*.

Of the 11 giant marlin that Mike Levitt takes in 14 days, two are granders and one of them weighs 1,058 pounds. One blustery afternoon off Ribbon Reef No. 7, Mike demonstrates not only his great dedication to the sport, but also his great sportsmanship.

The seas are lumpy, as they usually are; the sky is gray and threatening, as it often is during the month of October—spring in Australia can be a time that the baitfish disappears in a swirl of spray and the cockpit becomes a madhouse as Mike free-spools the line off his reel, making sure there is no backlash, and makes ready to set the hook. Captain Whelan drives the boat forward, hollering, "Lock up! . . . It's a big one." Levitt straps into the fighting chair, braces himself as line pours off the big reel and smoke curls from its rapidly overheating drag.

Soon he turns the giant fish. "It's coming up!" a crewman shouts, and 100 yards off the stern, the monster breaks water, accompanied by a geyser that competes with Yellowstone Park's Old Faithful. The fish is a big—make that, mammoth—black marlin, bigger than any of us has ever seen. Within 30 minutes, it is within gaffing distance and Mike is yelling to the captain that it's over 1,500 pounds.

But before they can wire it, the fish dives and the fight is renewed. Then it is at the boat again. Mike clearly says, "I don't want to kill it unless it's over fifteen hundred."

The captain hesitates. The fish is much larger than any taken this week, including Skip Levitt's 1,103-pounder that was caught the day before. But is it bigger than 1,500? The captain cannot be sure.

"If we're not sure, stick a tag in it," Mike says. "Next year, it will be bigger. I've already taken one over a thousand, and that's enough, unless it's a new record."

The all-tackle record on 130-pound-class line is 1,560 pounds, set at Cabo Blanco, Peru, in 1953, by Alfred Glassell Jr. But according to captains who have caught numbers of big fish, the dimensions of that record effort do not correspond with its weight. Its length and girth, they contend, suggest a fish closer to 1,300 pounds, a mark that has been topped by several anglers, including Jo Jo Del Guercio of Fort Lauderdale, Florida, who landed a 1,323-pound black marlin while based on the same mother ship as we are.

Stu's Australian-trip host Mike Levitt battles his first 1,000-pounder.

(An aside to the Glassell marlin is the fact that he had a professional movie photographer on the boat with him the day the catch was made. The fish was played unusually close to the boat, and the footage so good that it eventually made its way into the movie version of Ernest Hemingway's *The Old Man and the Sea*. This despite the fact that a couple of Peruvian mountains can be seen in the background in a couple of the frames. Despite months of trying, the Hollywood film crews were never able to get footage as good as the Glassell, hence a deal was made and it was used. Watch the Spencer Tracy version of *The Old Man and the Sea*, and you'll see Glassell's marlin.)

An entry for the 80-pound-class record was held briefly this year by Steve Zuckerman of Los Angeles, an old friend I introduced to light-tackle fishing during the three months I was at Piñas Bay, Panama, in 1965. Steve's marlin weighed 1,232½ pounds, eclipsing D. Mead Johnson's previous mark by 14½ pounds, but was itself beaten only a few weeks later, on November 8, 1977, when Georgette Douwma, of London, brought in a 1,323-pounder on 80-pound-class line to claim the world record. Steve notched another record, however, which may not be beaten for some time: He became the only angler to land two 1,000-pounders in one day, and what makes that an even more outstanding catch is that they were both caught on 80-pound line.

His record fish, Steve said, fought hard for only a short time, diving deep under the boat before giving up after 20 minutes. But during that time, the fish charged the boat and ran its bill right through the bilges. The boat limped in for repairs and the weighing ceremony.

Damage to boats is an accepted hazard from the monster billfish. Del Guercio's charter boat suffered a smashed transom from one maddened marlin. Because it was only about a 400-pound fish, the crew had decided to tag it—when the fish turned the tables. It charged its attackers and rammed its blunted spear up through the transom door, into the sill, causing havoc among the crew and providing a kind of grisly humor. "Grab a hammer," one of them yelled, nearly hysterical, "and bend that damn thing over! Then we'll have the bugger."

The huge marlin spike, however, is no joking matter. People have been impaled on them and knocked senseless with one powerful swipe. The bill on a 1,000-pound marlin is more than 4 feet long, tapered from its 18-inch base to the thickness of a man's arm, and terminating in a blunted railroad spike. The bill is an awesome weapon the marlin uses as deftly as any musketeer wields a sword.

A big-game fishing moment of truth comes when the first deckie (mate) reaches for the wire leader to boat a black Marlin that might be a 1,000-pounder (grander).

Our charter boat, *Yanu III,* launched only a month before, already has two broken marlin bills in her hull. One marlin, a 700-pounder when boated, displayed a broken bill segment in its side. A vicious weapon, the spear commands the respect of the most swashbuckling crew. Even the average tiger shark, which inhabits the same tropic waters, gives the marlin its due.

Marlin often feed by zooming in and knocking the bait down with their bills. They then come back and swallow it headfirst. Their maw is a straight pipe from mouth to stomach, and though they seem to prefer small scad of about 2 pounds, marlin can easily wolf down a 15-pound tuna in one gulp.

Speaking of scad, it's the favorite bait food of even the largest marlin. Similar to our mackerel, scad are caught each morning on rod and reel by the Australian boat crews and anglers in anticipation of the afternoon's fishing, when marlin bite best. Rigged so they swim naturally on the surface, dive, and then swim again, the scad will induce marlin to bite when they have not shown interest in other baits.

In late afternoon, the boats troll scad on one outrigger and a large bait, maybe a 25-pound wahoo or yellowfin tuna on the other. Another bait, a mackerel-like fish called the tanguigue, is used for baits up to 20 pounds. The large bait attracts the quarry's attention, but they invariably strike the scad first. Scad are smaller and they seem to attract other fish when trolled. Those fish, "the razor gang" as the crew calls them, consist of 100-pound wahoo and tanguigue that will zoom in and chop the bait right behind the hooks. Some days, we have at least 15 razor chops while stalking giant marlin. But at 5:45 one afternoon, as I hopefully monitor my 8-pound bonito bait, a huge fish comes greyhounding in and crashes the bait in a streaming mountain of spray, its whole body pulsing livid fluorescent blue.

"Keep as much string on the reel as you can."

The cockpit becomes bedlam as I free-spool the line on the drop-back, lock up, and set the hook. It's not my favorite way of fighting fish, as I'd rather stand up and hold the rod, but I slide into the big fighting chair and buckle on the harness.

The chair is greased with soap so that as I flex my legs against the footrest, the fish is pumped forward and my backside slides to and fro in the chair. I move forward rapidly and retrieve line as I slide and then I shove backwards with my legs as on a weight lifting machine. Strong legs are a big factor in fighting the monster fish, and so are strong wrists and arms when winding back 300 yards of line time after time. In marlin fishing, as well as in any other type of fishing, one key to winning is to stay as close as possible to the fish.

Sometime during the fight, giant marlin, just like bonefish, tarpon, or any other hard-fighting game fish, will briefly make a mistake. Bewildered, it may pause and give you a chance with the gaff. If you are close enough to the fish, you can take it. As phrased by famous Australian marlin captain Peter Bristow, "Keep as much string on the reel as you can."

If, on the other hand, the fish has gotten a distance away, it may rejuvenate before you can retrieve that line. Recovered, the fish will fight on and on. Then it can be a matter of adept boat handling to intercept the fish. The captain may turn the boat and run after a hot fish or back down on one that is close.

My marlin makes its mistake within 15 minutes, and while it lies at a standstill next to the transom, alternately pulsing its violet blue colors and fading silver, I crank the swivel to the rod's tip-top. The wireman grabs the heavy leader with his gloved hand to haul the fish in close enough to gaff.

Wiring is one of the most dangerous and thrilling aspects of marlin fishing. The wireman grips the leader between thumb and forefinger with the palm of his hand toward his face, and takes a wrap around his hand. He hauls that in, muscling the huge fish an arm's length closer, then grabs a wrap with the other hand. From 30 feet out, the leader length, the fish is towed into gaff range. Sometimes all hell breaks loose. The fish may surge anew, creating a serious threat to angler and crew. Twenty-odd feet of heavy piano wire zinging across a slippery deck, coiling and snapping at the pull of a 1,000-pound fish, can amputate an arm or leg or even decapitate an unlucky victim. Wire clippers are an essential safety feature.

My fish, docile after 15 minutes, becomes a hellion two minutes later on the wire, nearly tearing off the first deckie's gloved hand and arm. "It's not a good fish unless you feel the blood run down your arm," he mutters as he grudgingly lets it go, and soon I have it close enough to wire again.

Eventually landed, the fish weighs 996, just four pounds short of the grander goal. Am I disappointed? I'll say not! The main reason for my being on the Great Barrier Reef is to shoot a film, so I fished for marlin a total of only one hour the whole trip. Even so, I am fortunate enough to tag and release one fish that weighs about 400 pounds and land a 996-pounder. Where else in this world can a fisherman go and fish for one hour and catch two marlin, one weighing nearly 1,000 pounds?

Ron Jones, Mike's state-of-the-art skipper, takes a turn at wiring an 800-pounder for Mike Levitt. No stranger to big fish, Ron is the captain of the boat off Cape Hatteras that landed a record 1,128-pound blue marlin on 80-pound-class line.

In our 14-day string, we have 93 marlin up behind the bait, and of those, we tag and release 37. Four are boated, three weighing over 1,000 pounds. The smallest is estimated at 200, while the largest, Mike Levitt's grand release, goes over 1,300 pounds.

Jo Jo Del Guercio, one of the finest conventional-tackle fishermen in the world, fishes 21 days and takes four marlin over a grand, his largest 1,323. Jo Jo also tags six fish estimated to be between 950 and 1,050, and lands a total of 77 marlin. Other anglers report similar results to confirm Cairns as one of the planet's most fertile big-fish grounds.

The Great Barrier Reef is in the Coral Sea, where the great marlin migrate, beginning at the northern tip of the Australian continent at Thursday Island, and curling down to the Tropic of Capricorn. Prime marlin fishing extends southward from Lizard Island, about halfway down along the Ribbon Reefs to Cairns. Between those two settlements is Cooktown, a major restocking port for fishing boats.

While there are some day trips that go out the 30 to 40 miles from Cairns to the reef, the ideal arrangement for giant marlin is to fish on one boat and live on another. A mother ship is used by many anglers, and ours was the *Ulysses,* an 85-foot, one-year-old, fully air-conditioned, and fully provisioned ship. It welcomed us after each day of fishing with hot showers, great food, a chance to stretch our legs as well as hobnob with the crew of another boat also anchored nearby. This arrangement allows the fishing boat to stay only 15 minutes from the best fishing grounds, and provides ultimate comfort for the guests. When necessary, the mother ship can also steam into Cooktown for provisions while the fishing boats continue stalking marlin.

Cairns itself is a city of about 100,000 people with numerous parks and beaches, some of them catering to nude bathers (sorry I missed that!) and the resort trade. The northernmost major center on the coastal highway, Cairns is also important in the sugar trade. But its springtime and life revolve around the giant marlin fishery.

Getting to Australia as well as fishing there is expensive. And, unfortunately, only those who have more than several thousand dollars to spend can hope to manage it. For example, airfare alone to Sydney is about $1,500 from most points in the United States. At Sydney, you must figure on staying overnight before going on to Cairns, and also returning. It's more than 1,000 miles, and you must stop at Brisbane to change planes.

The Australian people are among the world's finest and most accommodating, who, not unlike those in a Montana small town, cannot do enough for strangers. Even the taxi drivers are first rate, their meters registering in pennies.

The food is excellent, with restaurants of all types. Australian wines are second in my mind only to the finest California wines, and the Australian XXXX beer is an experience in itself.

Coming and going, you cross the International Date Line, so that even though you lose a day on the way out, you gain it coming back. You arrive home the same day you leave Australia after at least 18 hours en route.

Other fishing inducements exist for me besides black marlin. A fish called a barramundi resembles our snook, averaging 20-plus pounds and reaching well over 50 pounds. The barramundi will take topwater plugs, flies, popping bugs, and jigs. In addition, there is some of the finest, unknown rainbow trout fishing south of Sidney in the Snowy Mountains.

I've always said I'd like to fish for giant marlin on light tackle, particularly the fly rod. Unfortunately, on this trip the seas are too rough even to think about it, since in rough water there is too much separation between fish and boat in the swells, which increases the danger of break-offs.

Of course, all of us are intrigued with the idea of being the first to land the legendary 2,000-pound black marlin. It is an idea that is hard to dismiss, which is why I've repeated it as often as the pursuit of the 200-pound tarpon on fly—a feat, incidentally, that finally occurred. But back to Australia and black marlin, I saw some tremendous fish there, much larger than any we caught and surely over 1,500 pounds.

California's Kay Mulholland reportedly hooked the largest fish her captain had ever seen in Australian waters, but finally cut it free after an eight-hour battle that lasted into darkness. Angler Neville Green landed a fish that was half eaten by sharks, and its remains weighed in at 1,463 pounds. Peter Bristow, the charter boat skipper of whom I've spoken about in this book, has lost count of the granders he has taken himself. But he has seen five or six, he says, that are "monsters, horrible monsters."

Indeed, the fabled two-grander black marlin is out there, lurking off the Great Barrier Reef. Catching it is only a matter of time, and money.

The Boga-Grip gets into the action with a
nice striper at Martha's Vineyard.

Wandering for Linesides

Pursuing striped bass up and down the Atlantic coast can be as rewarding for the fly rodder as it is frustrating.

One year not too long ago, Flip Pallot and I made arrangements to go to Alaska to do a TV show on Pacific salmon, then fly over to the Kamchatka Peninsula of Russia, doing a second show on large steelhead trout for Flip's *Walker's Cay Chronicles.*

This trip had been set up during the month of August, good fishing in Alaska and prime fishing on Kamchatka. Less than a week before our departure, the Russian government decided it would not allow Alaska Airlines to fly into the Kamchatka Peninsula. Flip had a film crew set to go, and he needed to do a show.

We discussed different options, and he liked my suggestion of trying for a striped bass program in the northeastern part of the United States. I set to work trying to set up our venture by calling my friend Dave Beshara in Salem, New Hampshire. I explained our problem. We would need a good guide, a second boat, and accommodations for eight people, during one of the busiest times of the year on very scenic Martha's Vineyard. Dave managed to get in touch with Moe Flaherty, one of the all-time great striped bass guides on the Vineyard.

Moe not only changed his bookings to accommodate the show, but he also located a large mansion-type house with enough bedrooms and bathrooms to accommodate all of us. The big-fish run was long past, Dave said, but he could guarantee a multitude of small stripers—on flies. We wanted big ones, but small stripers on flies would be better than none at all.

This is the classic example of the importance not only of going to the right place to fish, but being there at the right time. We did catch lots of schoolies averaging 5 pounds in some of the rips, on just about every cast. Not too bad for fast-action fishing with lots of doubleheaders, but not the size we would like to show the TV audience.

Both Flip and I were set up with 8-weight rods, Flip was using a popping bug with a floating line, giving it a hard noisy pop, then letting it sit for a moment before starting a medium-fast, gurgling-type retrieve. I was using a sinking-tip line with a streamer fly. Not so visible to the TV viewing audience but much more effective in numbers of fish hooked and landed.

Unfortunately, we are not always able to pick the time of year to fish a particular area, unless we live there. If I was able to pick the time of year to fish Martha's Vineyard, my choice would be during the first couple weeks of June or the last couple weeks of September, when the bigger fish are migrating through the area. These are striped bass that run between 15 and 35 pounds and are a formidable fly rod fish.

Like many of our game fish, striped bass are migratory, wintering as far south as Georgia and South Carolina, spending their summer and fall following the food source of menhaden, herrings, shad, sand eels, anchovies, lobster, crabs, and shrimps to as far north as Nova Scotia.

Like my favorite fish, tarpon, they are basically school fish, and during their migration they often feed voraciously on both the incoming and outgoing tides, resting close to the bottom during the slack tide.

Fly fishing for striped bass started as early as the 1940s and seems to have reached a peak in the early 1970s when, due to pollution and commercial overharvesting, the fish numbers experienced an extreme decline. Then, during the early 1980s there was enough of a resurgence in the fishery to have thousands of anglers break out their fly rods, light spin-casting rods, and purchase boats small enough and light enough to get into the shallow areas and sight fish for these magnificent fish.

Some states, like Massachusetts, still permit the commercial harvesting of way too many thousands of pounds of striped bass per year. The Coastal Conservation Commission and Striped Bass Unlimited Organization have attempted to lobby the legislatures, not unlike the way we did in the State of Florida for snook, to: (1) set meaningful slot limits; (2) have all coastal states unify their regulations, establishing successful control and management of an extremely important financial fishery; and (3) establish Game Fish status, a move that, I've been told, has also cropped up from time to time and is met with stiff opposition from both recreational and commercial factions, preventing any legislation from getting off the ground.

When they first come in during their migration, they are lean and very aggressive. Their mind-set is to forage where the food source is plentiful. Places like the east side of Martha's Vineyard when the salt ponds are opened to the ocean and the balled-up bait within these ponds start flowing out to the ocean with the current. It's a great place to be, fly rod in hand, when the big fish start gorging themselves.

It's a well-known fact that striped bass are native to the Atlantic Coast. A fact that is not so well-known is the striper was transported across the country in one of the early transcontinental trains to San Francisco Bay in 1882, where they thrived beyond expectations. By 1935, the Pacific Coast striper, maintaining its migratory habits, could be found from Southern California to Oregon.

Around that time, the sport fishermen of California were starting to show interest in the striper. And well ahead of the Atlantic striper states, the Cronin-Fisher-Andreas Bill was passed, putting the striper on record as a game fish with no commercial fishing allowed.

Dave Beshara with another fly rod striper at Martha's Vineyard.

Striper history on the Atlantic Coast has been strange. During the late 1800s, the striped bass clubs along the New England coast were strongholds of the business tycoons of the day. Then, quite suddenly, due to pollution or just a cycle of nature, between 1900 and 1936, the striped bass all but disappeared from this portion of the Atlantic Coast.

Chesapeake Bay is a major spawning ground for striped bass as well as a playground for millions of people. It seems that the best catches for both small schoolies and the heavyweights happen around the Chesapeake Bay Bridge-Tunnel and shoals off Virginia Beach during November and December, probably during their southerly migration

The South Carolina and Georgia coastlines share an offshore area that is practically virgin. I have caught 15- to 20-pound striped bass in the river systems of both states while fishing in Redbone Tournaments for cystic fibrosis during the months of October and November. Talk about a surprise and a hard-hitting wild fight. You're using spinning tackle with 6-pound-test line, ¼-ounce bucktail jig, figuring on hooking a 1- or 2-pound trout or possibly a 3- or 4-pound redfish. Suddenly you're almost getting spooled by a bull 18-pound striper.

The future of these magnificent fish is still unknown.... Unless state governments cross the commercial fishing lobbyist line and do as we have done with snook in the great fishing State of Florida, creating slot limits, daily angler catch limits with closed seasons during spawning times, the future will be dim indeed for striped bass.

WAHOO'S! 10/12/75
S.W.F.R.A. RECORDS
15# TIPPET - 20#2oz
12# " - 15#4oz
9# " - 16#8oz
#" - 17-10oz

Wahoo Burning Rubber

When fish were given the need for speed, wahoo got in line twice!

What's the fastest fish that can ever swim away with your fly in its mouth? Bonefish? Steelhead? Salmon? Permit?

Actually, it's none of the above.

Nothing quite compares with the electrifying run of a hooked wahoo when it screeches away with your fly. Pound-for-pound, length-for-length, no other fish has that all-out rocket acceleration like the electric-silver-blue wahoo. They can peel off line as though you have an unlimited spool and they want it all.

Among the drag racers of the sea, the wahoo has to outrank such speedsters as bonefish, permit, sailfish, and marlin. If fish left rubber marks, wahoo would need a new set of tires after every encounter. And that alone is enough to make a serious saltwater fly rodder's mouth water in anticipation.

Imagine how I felt then, perched in the stern of a 24-foot boat, with 50 feet of fly line coiled in a bucket at my feet, as I tried to corral one of those master dragsters on a fly rod. The year was 1975, and only one other angler to my knowledge had caught a wahoo on a fly rod. Gil Drake Jr., registered a saltwater fly rod world record for 10-pound tippet in 1967, a 12-pounder. The fact that hardly anyone had ever done it before was enough to light my fire.

Facing. Bob Griffin congratulates Stu on having set four line-class, fly-rod-tippet world records in one day at Bob's Club Pacifico Fishing Resort.

A speedy, striped wahoo brought to the boat and gaffed.

The island of Coiba, where Club Pacifico used to be, offered the ultimate in almost any kind of light tackle hook-up, but especially wahoo, which muscled into the passes from July to November in numbers you could almost walk across.

So there I was, courtesy of Club Pacifico's owner Bob Griffin, who had made me a proposition I could hardly refuse. By long-distance phone call, Bob had told me the wahoo were as thick as fleas on a fox, and he thought he had the formula for getting them to take a fly.

Numerous world-renowned fly fishermen had tried to take one, without success. That was a challenge I couldn't resist. Also, back then, I had the good fortune to work as a pilot flying for Pan Am. I was able to grab the jump seat on a 727 from Miami to Panama.

The eyesight of the wahoo makes it a finicky eater. Its speed allows it to run rings around your bait or lure, giving it the once-over. The real problem, then, was centered on how to use a fly the fish would think attractive, and keep it moving fast enough to excite the fish into striking. That's where Bob Griffin's secret came in.

Bob rigged a 3-ounce lead-head feather with a size 7/0 hook and dropped it off the stern, on a 50-foot length of ½-inch nylon line attached to a heavy rubber bungee, to take up the shock of the strike. Then we trolled the feather behind the fast-moving boat, to see if we could attract a wahoo. I stood at the stern, fly rod in hand, with coils of fly line dumped into a bucket at my feet, ready for the experiment.

The striped lightning flashed onto the feather and in an instant had hooked itself. The boat mushed to a halt and I cast the fly into the area where the hooked wahoo was thrashing back and forth. I was using a blue-and-white Mylar divided-wing tarpon streamer on a size 4/0 hook. I stripped line in as fast as I could manage, double hauling, moving rod and line in opposite directions.

The strike came in a splashing, slashing jolt, and in a split second the coils of line at my feet zipped through the guides, sizzling as the fish made its electrifying first run. When the free line was gone, the surge of the fish on the free-spooling reel created a giant bird's nest of a backlash, with the fish still going. In a flash, the 10-pound leader snapped and the line when slack. The wahoo was gone, but it had shown us the feat was possible. The wonderful wahoo could indeed be taken on a fly rod.

We tried again, and in seconds another wild-eyed drag racer was burning the guides of my 10-weight fly rod with its initial charge. It peeled fly line and 80 yards of backing off, then turned a 90-degree corner, zooming off sideways. The thrill of that greased lightning run on a sensitive fly rod was like holding electricity in your hand. But as the fish neared the stern, it stopped, thrashed, and spit the tarpon streamer right back at me.

That was just the start of it. Three more times that day I brought fish to the stern only to have the hook pull out. By the time the sun went down, I was grinding my teeth in frustration. But tomorrow was another day.

That night I spent hours rigging tackle, building leaders in 15-pound class, 12-pound class, 10-pound class, and even 6-pound class mono, tied to a #2 coffee-stained leader wire.

My plan was to use a 10-weight, high-density-sinking, small-diameter, 30-foot shooting head, backed with 150 feet of monofilament, tied to the 30-pound-test Dacron backing on my Fin-Nor #3 wedding cake fly reel. My tackle was all ready for a predawn launch.

The first fish was on before the sun had become a circle in the sky. The fish screamed away, and this time everything worked. It barreled past, did a right-angle turn, then dived 60 feet down and circled the boat. I pumped it up, and in a couple of minutes it was in the boat, to my knowledge only the second wahoo ever to be legitimately caught on a fly rod. It weighed 16½ pounds on 10-pound-class tippet. Bob Griffin was as ecstatic as I, since it was another record for his Club Pacifico as well. We rigged again, with 12-pound-class tippet.

In less than an hour, another wahoo had snatched the fly and headed for China with it, and my reel was hissing as line was gobbled by the blue water behind the flashing neon dragster. Then it turned and came back to us, putting a huge bow in the line, and lots of slack. I reeled frantically to retrieve line, and soon the fish was boatside, and on the gaff. It was a 15½-pound wahoo that would be entered in the 12-pound-class tippet category. Two records down, and it wasn't yet noon. If I

could catch a wahoo on 6-pound-class tippet, there would be a chance to set all four tippet-class records in one day.

Knowing how much water resistance 30 feet of shooting head creates, the lightninglike speed the wahoo achieves would be too much for such a light tippet. I had built a fly line out of 10 feet of lead-core line, just long enough to cast. This would give a very low profile in the water, without too much line drag.

Even so, the first fish broke off after a 20-minute fight. The second fish broke off just after I cleared the mono running line. The third made classic moves for 30 minutes then dived deep. Gingerly I pumped it up, and breaking water, it went on a swift but short run, then came right to us. At 4:30 P.M., October 12, 1975, the wahoo weighed in at 17 pounds 10 ounces, to become the IGFA 6-pound-class record, which stands this day.

Now there was no stopping us. We sped back out and dropped the bungeed rig over the side. A bigger wahoo slugged it, and the captain stopped the boat. I quickly cast the fly, using a 15-pound-class tippet, and hooked up immediately. In a world record anticlimax, I managed to land a 20-pound wahoo in under ten minutes. We were back at the scales so quickly, the staff thought we had come in because we forgot something.

In a day that had literally been "one for the books," we took four world record wahoo in all four fly rod tippet classifications and wrote a how-to chapter on a fish that only one other angler had been able to catch on a fly.

Facing. Happy smiles all around as Stu and a young Panamanian Captain hold up the last of the four fly-rod record wahoos he landed in one day.

Flip Pallot lip-gaffed this would-be world record tarpon, revealing a previous shark wound.

When Terror Stalks the Flats

*It's a bloody affair when sharks attack your hooked tarpon
or bonefish. And sometimes it's downright dangerous!*

Nature's most effective and feared killers, sharks are a constant menace
to anything in the sea. But some species seem to favor tarpon as prey.

Great hammerheads and bull sharks hover near schools of tarpon wherever
they are found around the world, particularly along migration routes and
spawning grounds. When a tarpon feeding frenzy occurs, sharks become a danger—
not only to the fish but to man as well if he gets in tiburón's way.

Several years back, Lee Wulff and I were filming a *CBS Sports Spectacular* TV
show on tarpon fishing. Suddenly I see a shark rush in at a tarpon Lee has hooked.
The intruder is a greater blacktip, an 8-footer, lean and fast. It is the same shark that
is popularly known as a spinner shark.

Lee quickly breaks off his fly leader to give the tarpon a chance to escape. The
fish is not exhausted and appears to have enough energy left to elude the predator's
fearsome serrated teeth. The blacktip rockets in so fast that the outcome is inevitable.
It slashes a big chunk out of the tarpon with one bite.

Writer A. W. Dimock, who recorded his catches of tarpon from a canoe in the early
1900s, recalls times when big sharks eyed his frail craft as though they were trying to
decide whether to attack the hooked tarpon or Dimock himself. Dimock said he felt,
more than once, that sharks had measured him for a meal.

A 14-foot hammerhead shark grabs the estimated 100-pound tarpon near the boat.

Another famous Keys guide, Capt. George Hommell, Jr., was guiding a young female customer along tarpon alley behind Big Torch Key when a giant tarpon hit. Estimated at 200 pounds, the fish would surely be a new women's world record on 20-pound-class line. After a long fight, the tarpon had come close, and George was poised to sink the gaff home.

Just then, a tremendous hammerhead 18 feet in length came rushing up the channel between the flats. Without hesitation, it nailed the tarpon at the boat, shearing off one third of the big fish with one bite. The giant hammerhead spun around and swam back to the bottom to swallow that portion.

George, as shocked and disappointed as his client, asked if she would like to have the rest of the fish—the head and remainder of its gigantic body—to mount as a memento. She said yes, so George began to lift it into his 16-foot skiff before the hammerhead could get to it.

The shark roared back. It slammed into the boat's bottom with its back. Then it raised up alongside them, looking wildly, its eyes apparently searching for the rest of its fish.

George, fully aware of the danger from a shark that was bigger than his boat, figured it was time to get the hell out of there. He hit the starter button to fire up his 40-horsepower engine. But the hammerhead, not to be put off, grabbed the whirring propeller in its teeth and stalled the engine. Throwing the outboard in gear, Hommell hit the starter button again, and once more the shark clamped down on the prop. The third time, George revved the engine to high speed, hit the starter, and leaped away, getting the boat on plane immediately to escape the snapping jaws. He raced directly across the channel to a shallow mud flat and ran up high and dry.

The hammerhead hung around for 45 minutes, cruising back and forth, still trying to figure a way to get the rest of the fish. Blood streamed from its mouth from the propeller cuts, but that didn't deter it. The shark was ready to do battle with whatever had taken its tarpon.

Science has yet to come up with a good teleological explanation for the head design of one of nature's monstrosities, the hammerhead shark. Its family includes several different species (the common, great, and bonnethead) and they are found in warm oceans all over the world. The great hammerhead stretches to 18 feet or more, according to fishing guides who have measured the size against their skiffs. In the 1940s, when commercial fishing for the vitamin A found in shark livers was big business, the hammerhead was highly prized. Its enormous liver was worth as much as $500.

Whenever I see a hammerhead shark, I know there will be tarpon around, too. Hammerheads follow the schools of tarpon. Apparently, they detect the silver king's scent. Sharks have the most highly developed olfactory organ of any fish.

A hammerhead or bull shark ready for a meal will harass a school of tarpon by swimming around and around it until they have forced the fish into a milling ball. The shark will smash into this concentration of fish, trying to injure one with its head or body or rake its teeth across one. It will pick up the scent of the wounded fish immediately. Swinging its head back and forth to locate the source, the shark will dog the injured tarpon as long as necessary—even 24 hours or more—until it wears down its prey and rushes in for the kill.

It takes a lot of fuel to keep a 1,000-pound shark going, so a 100-pound-plus tarpon makes a fine meal.

Bull sharks, greater blacktips, duskies—all are hell on tarpon. The dusky shark is primarily a pelagic, deepwater fish that ranges from Africa to the Gulf of Mexico and New England, but it frequently swims right into the shallow flats after the schools of tarpon. A bluish gray on the back and white on the underside, the dusky reaches as long as 9 feet and weighs up to 500 pounds. A dusky will attack swimmers and is not scared off by a dozen humans.

Sports fishermen in Central America as well as in the Keys lose tarpon by the dozens to aggressive bull sharks. While not so agile as hammerheads, they are more aggressive.

At one time, I was guiding Ray Donnersberger, trying for a fly rod tarpon in the Metropolitan Miami Tournament. He was playing a very large one, around 150 pounds, in the Bahia Honda area of Florida Bay, when a big bull shark slashed in.

I cranked up the engine and ran toward the shark, hoping to scare it off. It moved away but came back immediately to harass the tarpon. I brought out my .38 revolver and put several slugs near it, but the big bull kept coming back. Finally, it brushed Ray's leader and broke off the fish. The tarpon zoomed away then. We never found out if it escaped.

A man named R. P. Straughan followed a big tiger shark in his little skiff off Miami a few years back, staying over it as the shark cruised along a shoal. The day was flat calm, so both adversaries could see each other clearly. Finally, the shark became irritated at the chasing game and swam off about 30 feet, turned, and charged. It smacked into the boat dead center and lifted the stern clear out of the water. Straughan hung on, not knowing what else to do. He was terrified as the shark made pass after pass, violently careening into the boat. Straughan ducked into the bottom. He thinks the shark finally left because it could no longer see him.

Charlton Anderson and a friend were fishing off the south coast of Florida when, without apparent provocation, a big shark rushed at their boat. It bit a hole in the bottom "as big as your head," according to Anderson. He stuffed a sweater into the hole and bailed furiously until they could reach shore.

Sharks have the strongest biting power of any fish in the sea, as strong as 18 tons per square inch. Yet most of them feed not by crunching, but by grabbing hold and wrenching their bodies sideways, chewing, using the powerful muscles of their tails to twist and turn their heads. The whole fish is designed to bite, hold, and rip chunks out of its victim.

Giant tarpon, even the biggest ones in the 200-pound range, are not a very good match for a bull shark or a hammerhead that weighs five times as much. Many tarpon are bitten in half the first time a shark gets close enough to snap its fearsome jaws.

Writers have been fond of endowing the shark with human attributes and thought processes, but the fact is that sharks are even dumber than most fish. The cerebrum, that portion of the brain we call the thought center, is highly developed in man and the great apes, and seems to get smaller in other creatures as the need for reasoning diminishes. Fish in general have a comparatively small cerebrum, and sharks have the smallest of all. They are, however, magnificently designed to fit their element, the sea, and to eat. Like other predators, they sense weakness in their prey, and never hesitate to move in when ready for the kill. They have been around, by some estimates, as long as 40 million years.

I would guess that sharks have harassed about 5 percent of all the tarpon I have caught. That doesn't mean, of course, that sharks were not around more often. They are not always ultra-aggressive.

Most fishermen are not really aware that a shark is after their tarpon until it's too late. Suddenly the fish is hit, and just as suddenly it's over. Occasionally, though, even the most rapacious sharks are cheated, and a tarpon will survive to fight another day.

Sharks will readily attack fish as you play them—tarpon, bonefish, everything. And a 14-foot hammerhead that is almost as long as the 17-foot boat can be a scary sight!

Not long ago, I was fishing with Flip Pallot, one of the country's top anglers and one of my best fishing partners, in the Sugarloaf Key area. Flip was poling at the time, and I was casting a fly to a very large tarpon. The fish took the fly, and I set the hook to begin a marvelous aerial battle. It jumped half a dozen times, ran all over the bay.

After about 35 minutes, I brought it to the side of the boat. Flip lip-gaffed it, a precaution that holds the fish but does not kill it. Then we noticed that this very large fish had a wide crescent of missing scales on its side. It had previously been shark-bit, but not during this fight, because the wound had begun to grow new tissue. A large glazed area had formed over it.

We guessed the attack had occurred two or three weeks before. The tarpon easily weighed more than 150 pounds. The bite area was as large as a garbage can lid. The shark had to be much larger than any hammerhead I have caught, considering the size of those jaws. Perhaps it was a great white—but, of course, I'll never know.

Flip and I decided not to kill the tarpon—even though it was potentially a world record—because of the controversy that might develop over the fish's fighting ability after the shark bite. Instead, we slipped the lip gaff out of its mouth and helped it recover. With a helping shove, it swam off, a lucky tarpon that not only escaped the worst predator in the sea but also survived an encounter with man.

Now, every spring when I see the first signs of the tarpon run, with big ones stacking up in the channels around Key West, I think of that big courageous silver king we let go.

I sure hope it's still out there somewhere.

Stu applying maximum pressure on an almost-beaten Pacific sailfish.

chapter 28

Light Tackle, Big Fish—My "Down and Dirty" Rules

In fresh or salt water, these six tips can help you land the fish you want the most—the big ones!

Whether you're fighting a big fish in fresh or salt water, the difference between success and failure can often be the amount of time required to land that fish.

In my experience, based heavily on big tarpon and other saltwater bullies like sailfish and permit, to play him long is to play him wrong!

I have six rules I try to follow to help me keep the fight short and sweet:

1. Your tackle must be in tip-top shape. When after big fish, I always have plenty of extra leaders rigged with proper 100 percent knots. If you're fishing for tarpon or billfish, it's important to have a leader stretcher with a variety of flies already attached to the leaders and ready to go. Also, make sure your hooks are as sharp as humanly possible.

2. After you cast your fly to a tarpon or billfish, it is important to place the rod butt in the center of your belly, slightly leaning forward, while pointing the rest of the fly rod down your fly line toward your fly. Move the fly by stripping line, *not by moving the rod tip*. If you see the fish eat your fly, wait until it closes its mouth before you set the hook. (It's one of the reasons this is called "sight fishing.") When you strike, keep the rod butt in the center of your belly; if you're

Notice the glove on Stu's left hand and the rod butt in the center of his stomach, with fingers on the line applying additional drag as needed.

right-handed, take that extra strip of line with your left hand as you rotate your body to the right, keeping the rod butt firmly in place. Pull sharply and securely with your left hand as you strike the fish while twisting your body and the rod in the opposite direction.

3. After setting the hook, look to the bottom of the boat or, if you're wading, around your ankles to see where the fly line is, to make sure that you're not stepping on it. Then holding it lightly but securely with the fingers of your line hand, make sure it comes off the deck without catching on anything. I have seen, and I have had, fly lines wrapped around various items in the boat and around many parts of my anatomy. Talk about Murphy's Law! This is prime time for line mishaps to occur.

4. When the fly line is cleared and starts coming off the reel, you can breathe again. There is little you can do while the fish makes its first run, so that's when I reach in my back pocket to get a left-handed cotton glove and put it on. (I'm right-handed.) The glove will act as my drag while I fight any big fish. The first finger of my left hand will guide the line back and forth evenly on the reel as I wind in line. My fingers can also add as much as 4 pounds of drag against the fish's mouth by squeezing the line. Then if the fish surges or jumps, I can release the drag from my fingers without breaking my tippet. Near the end of the fight, if I have to apply 12 to 15 pounds of drag, all I have to do is to place my gloved little finger around the line as well.

5. One of the most important rules to remember when fighting big fish is to get close to the fish as quickly as possible, and the only way to do that is to wind line as fast as you can, with your dominant hand. At numerous shows, I have demonstrated with a 15-pound-test Boga-Grip the reason it is so important to be close to your adversary when you are trying to apply pressure. I pick a volunteer from the audience to stand 20 to 30 feet away from the rod tip and hold the scale. I easily show that I can bottom out the scale at 15 pounds of drag at that distance, using the method just described. I then have that person move about 90 feet away, with all my fly line out. Pulling just as hard as I did against the scale when it was closer, I can pull only a maximum of 6 pounds. The stretching of the line disperses the rest of the energy I'm applying through the fly rod.

6. To really wind line fast, you must attack the handle at a 90-degree angle so you can crank it using only your wrist—just like with a pencil sharpener. I have heard various reasons from many trout fishermen and relatively new saltwater fly fishermen. Some say they want to pull on the fish with their strong arm, and some say they've been spin fishing most of their lives and are comfortable winding with their left hand. I'll begin with the first group first:

   You should never use your arms when pulling on big fish. Instead, keep your elbows tucked into your side and pull with your body. As an example, if the fish moves to the right, you should move your left foot to the left and move your shoulders and body to the left, thus letting your back and shoulders do the work—not your arms. If the fish faces directly away from you, put your right foot behind you and lift up. If it's truly near the end of the fight, turn your body sideways to the fish and pull down and to the right or down and to the left, always pulling toward the tail of the fish. This was the technique that I developed and perfected back in the 1960s on big tarpon and Pacific sailfish, and called "down and dirty."

   Now to address the new saltwater fly fisherman who spent many years using spinning tackle: Most believe they developed the ability to wind effectively with their left hand. What they fail to remember is the average spinning reel has a 4:1 or 5:1 retrieve ratio, while fly reels have a 1:1 retrieve ratio. That means you must turn the handle of the fly reel many more times to retrieve the same amount of line as with a spinning reel. Your less dominant hand will certainly tire faster.

As Mark Twain once said, "If I was a better writer, with a better vocabulary, I'm sure I could make this article much shorter."

I agree!

Above and facing. Jeff Harkavy shows proper technique fighting a big Pacific sailfish. Jeff's exuberance shows when the mate bills this fish before releasing it.

Scottie Yeager weighs her 96-pound Pacific sailfish caught with a top water plug, using a bass-fishing reel without any built-in drag.

chapter 29

A Sailfish Spectacle

*Battling Pacific sailfish with tackle meant for bass fishing
is more than a man's game. A day on the water with Scottie
Yeager goes in my memory bank as one of the best ever!*

One of my most-remembered days at Club de Pesca Panama (now Tropic Star Lodge) at Piñas Bay came with a lady angler in my boat. She was Scottie Yeager, one of the founders of the International Women's Fishing Association (IWFA). That day on the water with Scottie was a premier example of what it's like to take on Pacific sailfish with light tackle—the kind of tackle actually meant for largemouth bass fishing.

Scottie grew up in Florida, loving fish and fishing, and she was known as an outstanding conservationist. The day before, she has fished hard and expertly. On what has been an exceptionally rough and stormy day, she hooked, played, landed, and released seven of Piñas Bay's famed sailfish on 20-pound-class line. But she had broken into tears when we were unable to revive one of the fish and release it successfully.

When we head out the next day, a light wind ripples the surface, but otherwise the sea is calm. The moody tropical weather is on our side this very important July day. Soon after we leave the dock, the mate puts a ballyhoo over the side, and we troll it slowly over the sun-warmed water. There is no hook in the bait, as it has been rigged as a teaser to bring a sailfish to the surface so the caster can get a lure to it.

Scottie Yeager and the captain after the fish of her dreams is boated.

The governing rules of most fishing clubs like the International Women's Fishing Association are tough. The angler must cast the lure and retrieve it from a dead boat, which means a boat not under power. If the angler casts to a fish from a moving boat, it qualifies only as a trolling catch.

Scottie is armed with a 6½-foot fiberglass plug rod and an Ambassador 6000 plug-casting reel that I myself have modified to conform to the IWFA regulations. I have removed the anti-reverse mechanism and preset the drag so that it cannot be adjusted while a fish is being played.

The reel is loaded with 200 yards of 15-pound-test fluorescent monofilament. There is a 6-foot shock leader of 20-pound-test monofilament, to which is connected a short piece of wire. An oversized, ungainly looking chugger-type of wooden plug is attached to the wire leader.

Scottie is going to try to catch a Pacific sailfish on light freshwater casting tackle—a feat that only a handful of expert male anglers has ever accomplished.

Trolling baits with or without hooks can be a tiring and sometimes unrewarding method of fishing. It's possible to spend many long hours with nothing more to do than watch the baits skip across the sun-glistening surface of the water. During the first hour or two, it seems easy to stay alert, but after that, most fishermen start relaxing and are lulled into a sleepy state by the warm sun and the gentle rolling of the boat. But the top anglers stay aware of such moments and maintain a readiness, because many fish have been hooked only to get off the line because the anglers were too slow in responding.

Fortunately for Scottie, that doesn't happen today. A long dark shape suddenly materializes just under the surface and gains rapidly on the skipping ballyhoo teaser.

"Sail!" I yell, but Scottie has seen the fish, too, and is poised to cast. The skipper reduces speed and slides into neutral gear as the mate reels in the ballyhoo decoy. The hungry sailfish rushes aggressively at the teaser bait, but the mate deftly plays his part by keeping the decoy just tantalizingly out of its reach, drawing the fish ever closer to the stern of the boat.

"It's a beauty," I say as Scottie places the big plug within 3 feet of the now very frustrated sailfish. *Ka-pop, crash, splash!* Scottie works the plug almost violently, and the sail sees it and attacks in a fury of foam not 30 feet from the boat. Scottie slams the hooks home, and the stung fish takes to the air.

As the cobalt blue torpedo slashes at the surface, a veil of sunlit spray seems to hang in the salt air. The handsome head shakes in a desperate effort to throw the plug, its strength transmitted through the line to the straining anglerette.

The engine is in gear again and the skipper tries to keep up with the sailfish, but we are too slow and are losing distance. Still, the line holds. As the little rod that has really been designed for largemouth bass bends double, the fish leaps mightily and throws the plug.

A massive sigh in unison consumes the boat. Scottie retrieves the lure and I inspect the hooks for damage, but only a small piece of flesh has been torn from the sailfish's mouth.

Nonetheless, Scottie has hooked her first sailfish on plug-casting tackle. The mate rapidly puts another ballyhoo teaser over the side. Scottie remains alert, searching the water behind the bouncing, diving teaser through her green polarized glasses.

Another sailfish, a large one, comes right in on the bait. Everything goes like clockwork. When the teaser "escapes" the sail, it turns its fury on the big wooden plug, hitting it with its bill, trying to stun or kill it. Scottie's reflexes are spring-loaded and she strikes hard. The plug goes flying through the air and lands 20 feet away from the fish. The startled sailfish seems to look right at Scottie in disgust as it turns tail and runs.

Even so, Scottie is exhilarated. "Wow," she exclaims, "what a way to fish for sailfish!"

We lose that teaser bait to a yellowfin tuna that comes up without warning. I watch as another ballyhoo teaser is quickly put over the side. The interruption caused by the uninvited tuna is brief, as a pair of sailfish comes up from behind our wake.

"Yahoo!" I yell. "We must be at a sailfish convention."

Both fish want that bait badly, and the mate has a job keeping it away from them. It seems as if nothing will spook the two sails, and Scottie's plug lands in front of and between them. Both fish scramble for it, and the smaller fish wins the race, as is often the case.

When the fish grabs the plug, Scottie braces herself and strikes several times. Using every bit of timing and coordination necessary, she embeds the hooks into the hard mouth of the sailfish. The violence of the first few minutes of runs and jumps makes it seem as if the sailfish is trying to gain its freedom by making us cower from its show of force. But Scottie is still the master, and it isn't until the battle is halfway won that the hooks tear loose and this fish, too, is free.

Some say 13 is an unlucky number, but Lady Luck is like the weather—fickle and unpredictable. Scottie's 13th sailfish of the past two days is giving the mate fits. It darts from side to side, taking vicious, accurate swipes at the teaser. As the boat slows, I wonder how Scottie has strength enough left to cast, much less to play another fish. While those thoughts race through my mind, I watch in wonder as the big plug flies through the air and lands just alongside the sail's left eye. As if attracted by a magnet, the plug immediately becomes the all-consuming interest of the sailfish. It forgets the ballyhoo, and in anger and frustration, lunges at the plug.

Scottie sets the hook again and again. The sharp sting of hooks going through flesh and bone puts the sailfish into a frenzied leap only 40 feet from the boat. Scottie has her hands full, holding on to the little rod. Just keeping the rod tip high and giving enough slack by bowing to the fish when it jumps is a full-time job.

The skipper has the boat in gear again and does the best he can to keep Scottie from losing too much line. Leap after leap, jump after amazing jump, the sailfish puts on an aerial display that is ample reward for any fisherman. It tail-walks across the surface, throwing its dorsal from side to side. Scottie is determined to land this one, if only the line doesn't break and the hooks hold.

As if it received a second wind, the fish comes the last few feet to the surface with regained speed, and jumps twice. But the vigor it had before is lacking in these last jumps. Now the fish swims away from the boat, putting its shoulder into it, like a horse pulling a plow. It is taking line, but this time, only a little bit.

Scottie grits her teeth and begins a steady pumping. Now the tables are turned, and Scottie begins to steadily gain line. The fish looks beautiful as the sunlight reflects off its spread dorsal fin. Precious monofilament now fattens the spool, and the sailfish is only 20 feet from the boat. With two short, fast pumps, Scottie slides the sail within reach of the mate's waiting gaff. He strikes expertly and the fish thrashes and throws water all over us. The gaff holds, and the captain jumps down from the bridge to grab the sail by the bill.

We get under way as rapidly as we can, for we have some two hours of running before reaching the dock at Club de Pesca. Back at the dock, it is an extremely happy Scottie Yeager who watches the scale go up, up, and up to 90 pounds—a fantastic feat for anyone using that kind of tackle suited for fish less than one-tenth the size of that sailfish.

This time, Scottie is too happy and excited to cry. Her new IWFA record took her only 40 minutes. But what a fantastic span of time it has been. Scottie is all smiles as we shake her hand, and congratulations go all around.

That was the kind of fishing and dock scene that happened frequently in those early days at Club de Pesca Panama.

Stu joins in the congratulations after Scottie Yeager weighs in her 96-pound Pacific sailfish.

chapter 30

Behaving Yourself on the Flats: A Guide's Plea

*Etiquette, behavior—whatever you want to call fishing
manners—there are commonsense rules for every kind of fishing,
and in flats fishing, these are ones the good guys follow.*

Having had the opportunity to be on both ends of a backcountry skiff, as a
guide for many years and as an angler, I feel reasonably qualified discussing
what is proper etiquette from both points of view.

FROM A GUIDE'S POINT OF VIEW

To begin with, a backcountry skiff is a rather small (16- to 18-foot) area that
serves as the guide's office, sometimes more than 30 days in a row. Most good
guides like to work in a clean office and will have their skiff spic-and-span each
morning when greeting clients.

New clients will be getting off on the right foot (so to speak) if they wear soft-
sole boat shoes that will not leave black marks on the clean deck. It's nice to
ask the guide where they would like you to put any garbage or empty soft drink
cans, as most guides do have a specific place. While on the fishing grounds, open
and close any compartment lids as quietly as possible, and try not to make any noise
banging or kicking things in the boat. Guides take a lot of pride in producing fish for
their anglers, and noise can frighten the fish, wrecking his best efforts.

There were quite a few times that I shut off the engine in a deep channel, more
than a quarter of a mile away from the place I expected to find the fish. Sometimes

that involved poling into the wind and into the current in order to get the angler close to the still-undisturbed fish, only to have a second angler in the boat slam a compartment lid, spooking every fish within 100 yards. Talk about having a small space get even smaller in a hurry.

The evening before your trip is the time to discuss the type of fishing and species of fish you would prefer to catch if the weather conditions, tides, and time of year permit. This is also a good time to discuss what type of tackle, and how much tackle you should bring. There is only a minimal amount of storage space in most backcountry skiffs. Most anglers were more than happy to use my equipment, knowing that it would be properly rigged for the type of fishing they would be doing.

Be aware that the Florida Keys is the only place in the world that I know of where it is customary for the anglers to provide lunch for themselves and the guide. You might be shocked, but you heard me right: your lunch *and* the guide's. So you might ask your guide if he has any meal preferences.

Back in the early 1960s, I remember guiding for 100 days in a row. I can tell you that I got very tired of eating ham and cheese sandwiches the clients ordered without asking what I wanted for myself. I still remember fishing with some very nice people that were new to the Florida Keys and the local custom of providing lunch. When they broke out their sandwiches and saw I wasn't pulling out my own sack, they asked if I wasn't going to take time for lunch. They had not gotten the word about providing my lunch. Rather than embarrass them, I always replied, "No, I never eat lunch out on the boat."

FROM THE ANGLER'S POINT OF VIEW

It is not uncommon to have long-lasting friendships develop between the angler and guide. I believe these start with proper courtesy and etiquette toward each other.

The angler knows when the guide is working really hard in order to put him into proper position for the cast. This type of fishing is a team effort. You can bet that the angler also knows when he's made a bad cast that possibly spooked the fish, and feels very bad about not holding up his end of the team effort.

Guides who make sarcastic remarks—or even worse, like outright bitching—about poor casting aren't giving the angler the help he needs. It just might be time for the guide to critique the cast in a helpful manner.

It is not only good etiquette but also extremely important for both the angler and guide to know what they expect of each other. Some anglers say that they don't really care whether they catch fish or not. They just want to have a nice day. If that's really true, be sure to let the guide know as much before leaving the dock in the morning. Perhaps a little more flats sightseeing is in order, instead of a relentless pursuit of fish.

Producing fish is very important to most guides, and sometimes that goal may be too extreme for the abilities and desires of the client.

That's why it's important for both the angler and guide to be on the same page. That they both understand, and try to help with each other's problems. Wouldn't you call that good etiquette? I do.

Another way of handling an inconsiderate incident was told me by a dear friend, mild-mannered, soft-spoken Capt. Rick Ruoff. The story about a flats bully that I related back in chapter 1 of this book is nothing compared to what happened to Captain Ruoff.

Rick said he had a client bonefishing down a shoreline just east of Harry Harris State Park in Tavernier, in the Keys. It was a beautiful slick-calm morning with many schools of bonefish, and his client was getting numerous shots at them. Rick said he actually heard the Jet Ski before he saw it running down the shoreline toward him.

Putting his pushpole between his legs, using both arms, he motioned the Jet Ski to move out from the shoreline. Shooting him the bird, this Jet Ski driver commenced to do to complete figure eights around Rick, blowing all the bonefish off the flat.

Rick quickly poled his boat into deep enough water to drop his engine and start it, asking his angler to sit down and hold on. As he jumped on the plane at full throttle, Rick started slowly gaining on the Jet Skier, who probably made a mistake by heading out into the ocean. Just before Rick caught up with him, he leaped off his Jet Ski in a panic, and the kill switch immediately shut off its engine.

Without saying a word to the guy, who was now bobbing in his life jacket, Rick idled up to the Jet Ski, catching one of its handlebars under his boat's towing eye. Gunning his big engine, he snapped the handlebar off.

Rick came around for a second pass, this time doing a repeat performance on the other handlebar. Rick said he then pulled up to the Jet Skier, looked down at him in the water, and said, "If you ever do that to me again, that's what will happen to your arms."

Some people might consider this payback a little extreme, but many other fishermen would say Rick gave that man his just deserts.

Shows you, I guess, that direct action sometimes is more effective than diplomacy.

Showtime! It's Your Movie

*Want to make your own fishing movie for TV or
the Internet? These tips can help you get started.*

How would you like to star in a movie? Or be the producer and director of one
like you sometimes watch on those long winter Saturday afternoons, leaving
you dreaming about fishing in various corners of the globe?

have watched a number of them myself, usually with a certain amount of envy
for the guy who's holding the fishing rod. Sometimes the images on the screen
bring back my own stored-up memories of the location they're fishing.

But I've also done my share of filming and found it the perfect way to save a fishing
trip forever, to enjoy it again and again in the comfort of my living room. You can
do it, too.

All it takes is time and patience, some specialized gear, and also some luck to have
it all come together for an entertaining 20 to 30 minutes. With the proper planning
and organization, you'll end up with never-to-be-forgotten scenes in a movie that's
all yours. You're the producer, the director, and even the cameraman. Or perhaps
you'd like to star in the movie you produced and directed and have someone else on
the camera end. Like Clint Eastwood sometimes does.

Before you actually start filming, you have to realize that some fish are more
photogenic than others. Your film will be far more interesting if you're after a fish
that delivers a lot of action in runs, jumps, and color. It's important to have more
to show than just the angler bending the rod, tugging at the fish. We're talking fish

like tarpon, marlin, sailfish, snook, rainbow trout, largemouth bass, striped bass, or dolphin, to name a few. Scenes of feeding fish can add a lot of visual excitement. Tailing bonefish, permit, or redfish are one example. Stripers or bluefish attacking a school of baitfish is another. And you might be surprised by the jumps you get out of a smaller fish like pickerel.

Whenever possible, choose a location where the water is calm enough so the person with the video camera can focus on the fish while keeping a straight horizon. No one likes to get seasick in the boat or while watching a film where the camera person is rocking and rolling along with the boat.

It's as important to have backup camera equipment as it is to have backup fishing tackle. To give you a comparison with the pros, the television crew that used to shoot *The American Sportsman* series might plan to be on location for eight days, with two cameramen, a soundman, a producer-director, production manager, plus three boats to shoot from different angles at the same time. All that for a segment that would run only around 15 minutes on the weekly half hour show.

Of course, you're only one guy or gal, trying to make a show that is worth watching and conveys the excitement anglers feel when stalking and catching that big one. The main thing you must have is a storyline. From the first scene to the last, the film should tell the story of how someone went out and landed that prize catch. The angler's desire to catch that particular fish, the location, the challenges, the tactics used. All that must be *shown*—not just talked about, but *shown*—in the pictures.

But . . . this is very important . . . you don't tell a story like that from the beginning. There's a better way.

Some 30 or more years ago, I was producing and directing a TV show for Thrill Maker Sports at Parismina Tarpon Rancho in Costa Rica with Boston Celtics basketball great John Havlicek. We were planning on 100-pound tarpon and record-breaking snook that roam the river mouths, lagoons, and along the beach at a tropical paradise. I did have a loose storyline that told about traveling to Costa Rica, staying in a wilderness lodge, and catching as many big tarpon and snook as we could bargain for. Before it was over and the film "in the can" (we were using 16 mm sound cameras), we had caught plenty big fish, but not without the problems that can plague an on-location expedition.

To start with, even with a storyline, you shoot a fishing film backwards. You start from the end result, the catching of the fish, and go backwards from there. The reason for that is, obviously, if you don't catch fish, there is no story, no film. It may not be so easy as it looks on TV.

Fortunately, finding tarpon in Costa Rica was no problem whatsoever. The big, shallow areas just off the beach have migrating tarpon crowding in for most of the year. Many of them weighing more than 100 pounds.

For John Havlicek, however, catching one became a temporary problem. An excellent angler, John had never fished for tarpon and was not used to setting the hook in such a bony mouth, and then bowing to give slack when the silver king jumped. He lost an even dozen before he solidly hooked one and brought it to the boat. Even so, we got some good shots of the action at regular speed, and in slow motion. Slow mo, by the way, can sometimes be done during the editing now.

It's important to have plenty of charged batteries and memory sticks if you are doing digital, or tapes if you are not.

The secret to getting really professional jumps is to have the camera rolling before the fish comes out of the water. Then you should continue filming after the fish is back in the water, sometimes slowly panning from the fish, up the line to the rod, and to the angler before turning the camera off. The best filming includes a close-up of the water lumping up, then bursting as the fish leaps, soaring across the frame, and plunges back down again.

A few years earlier, I was doing an ABC's *American Sportsman* TV show on the Pacific side of Costa Rica with linebacker football great Dick Butkus. Dick had been fishing only once in his life, and that had been years before, with conventional 30-pound-test trolling tackle. When he told me about it on the phone, he seemed quite proud of the 10-pound snook he had caught trolling out of Marco Island, Florida.

Whether you're filming or just fishing, luck plays an important part in your success. And this would be Dick Butkus's first time ever using spinning tackle or fishing for big fish. Because of that, Dick did have at least six sailfish grab his artificial squid without being hooked. After each one, I would calmly explain what he had to do to properly set the hook. I told him that after the line came tight to make believe he was hitting someone with a series of sharp jabs. Only, instead of punching, he should be sharply jerking back with the rod.

A great athlete, Dick put my coaching to work on the next two sailfish, hooking and landing them both. That gave the two cameramen plenty of action jumps from different angles, and boat-to-boat landing shots of Flip Pallot billing both sails. I had invited Flip to join us and run the fishing boat that would be on camera during the shoot.

In the finished show, you only saw Dick fight and land one sailfish; the other sailfish ended up on the editing floor, as the saying goes. This film won a Teddy Award for being the best fishing program produced in the United States that year.

Notice that I used the expression "boat to boat." To make a really good video that tells a story, you need a second boat. You might get a few shots by being in the same boat as the angler, but to really get the film right, you'll have to be in a separate boat.

You don't need to have a big heavy video camera with a large zoom lens to make a good home video that will be enjoyed for many years. There are a number of small, lightweight digital cameras on the market today that will do everything you need to do while putting together a good show.

In deciding whether to have a hard drive– or card-type camcorder, be aware that the trend in video cameras is hi-def. Most of these cameras shoot to either an internal hard drive or some type of memory card. I recommend a camcorder that allows you to shoot to a card, which gives you the option of carrying multiple cards (three or four), giving you peace of mind that you will not run out of hard drive space while filming your wife's "First Tarpon Ever." It's also wise to have at least one extra battery.

Buying the best quality camcorder you can afford will be your first smart moviemaking move. Shooting at the highest resolution helps to keep you from having blurred images. Remember: the video you shoot today will become "moments in time" to be relived over and over again for many years.

There are four major brands—Sony, Panasonic, JVC, and Cannon. Each has its own pluses and minuses. Discounting professional models, there are two types to consider—"consumer" and "pro-sumer" models. The consumer models may be found in most retail stores but the "pro-sumer" models are found mostly via an Internet search. The "pro-sumer" models are going to cost more; however, they will have better quality and offer more features such as better lenses. And the lens is the bread and butter of shooting quality videos.

Most of today's camcorders are small and light, which offer a great advantage when traveling. However, the light weight can make the camera difficult to hold steady while shooting in the boat. A shoulder mount will help steady the camcorder, and a good external microphone with a wind muff will help produce better audio.

Editing your home video or movie, turning it into a real story instead of just a collection of scenes, is the final part of the process. The techniques and aids needed are beyond the scope of this article, but you'll find all the how-to and guidance you need on the Internet.

A Flats-Fishing Epic

The tarpon on the line is obviously a new fly fishing world record. But at six hours into the fight, neither contestant can claim victory.

It is early afternoon, late May 1980, in Homosassa, Florida. Capt. Hal Chittum and his client, Marvin "Mad Dog" Levine, scan the clear salt water at the daisy-chain circle of big spawning tarpon. They cannot believe their eyes. The armored monster in the center looks more than 8 feet long. Circling are a dozen 100-pound companions looking like drones attending their queen bee.

Chittum slowly shifts his pushpole and sucks in his breath. He has to have that fish. Levine, an expert with a fly rod, will try for it on 15-pound-test tippet. He takes careful aim with a false cast and presents his fly perfectly.

The big fish lunges, throwing up a bow wave that splashes away the tiny blue streamer fly. "Awesome," Hal gasps. Again the fish lunges, and misses. "Breathtaking." Hal's pulse is racing. The tarpon wheels for a third try, and Levine begins stripping in line, moving the fly in quick jerks. But Chittum yells sharply at him, "Stop! Stop the fly! Stop stripping! Let her take it. That's the biggest goddamn tarpon I've ever seen!"

The "biggest goddamn tarpon" comes on, unafraid, and closes its bucket-size mouth on the fly. Hal can no longer control himself. "Hit it!" he yells. "Hit it! Hit it! Hit it!"

Levine strikes it, two, three, four times. The fish shakes its huge head and takes off like a rocket. In an instant, it burns 250 yards of backing from the big Emery fly reel.

Hal guns the engine in pursuit, shouting, "I've never seen anything like this! I'm running thirty-five hundred rpm just to keep up. That tarpon is humongous." Visions of the legendary 200-pound-plus tarpon on the fly floods his mind. This one will go 250, even 300, and hang up the tarpon record forever.

It is a record Hal Chittum, superguide, wants more than any other: the first 200-pound tarpon on a fly. Although records themselves are nothing new to this big, affable young man, it will be his measure of immortality as a Florida Keys fishing guide. He is already in a class by himself. To date, Hal's clients own every major record for tarpon on a fly rod. It is a distinction no other guide can claim. Any expert angler will admit that guides were responsible for at least half the angler's fishing accomplishments.

With Hal, big tarpon are his specialty. No, more than that. They are an obsession, a personal goal driving him stronger than anything else in his life. In a business where a few hundred men make their living, his big-tarpon fever has made him rise to the top and be acclaimed and sought by some of the most accomplished anglers in the world.

Yet, Hal Chittum is only 28 years old. He has been guiding as a professional for less than six years. "It may be a short time as guiding goes," he observes, "but it wasn't always easy."

As a former guide myself, I know he's right. Going fishing every day in the paradise of the Keys for a $165 daily fee in the 1970s may sound like an ideal way to make a living, but it *isn't* easy. It's a game of expensive equipment and very specialized know-how. It's rigging tackle and tying leaders every night, rolling out of bed at 4 A.M. and poling a boat for hours at a time—damn hard labor. It's fighting and gaffing fish plenty big enough to hurt you. And it's a world of psychology, catering to clients who can be very demanding. And the bottom line is knowing where the fish are and what they are hitting, every day. It's 200 days of fishing a year just to break even. This is not a job for anyone out of shape or not passionate about fishing.

Like every trade, guiding has its experts and its also-rans, and a few, like Hal, who do everything well. His trademarks are the best in equipment, an intelligent approach to fishing, the physical strength to do the job, and a charming enthusiasm for his work. Ask him how he's doing, and he'll invariably come back with, "Excellent!"

Today his expertise, however, is a sharp contrast to the days back when Hal was a beginner. A big, raw kid, 6 feet 3 inches, 225 pounds, with only a little skill but a lot of burning desire, he was just out of college and in pre-law. Hal was accused of "wasting people's time and money," by other guides and anglers. "The bumbler," some called him.

But Hal was ambitious and determined. He spent a couple of years fishing on his own and learning from others about the fish, the tides, and the techniques. Eventually, some of his teachers began to value his services as a guide over all other guides, especially for saltwater fly rodding for tarpon.

Above, by aggressively thrusting the rod toward a jumping fish and creating some slack line, you have a better chance of keeping the fish from throwing the hook, and *below,* as they frequently do, this tarpon has turned completely upside down. Note the remora still attached to its side.

A variety of color patterns of the Original Apte Tarpon Fly. The yellow and orange pattern was featured on a U.S. postage stamp in 1991.

In the rarefied atmosphere of top-notch saltwater angling, the pinnacle of man against fish is the light-tackle, big game fish matchup, where 10-to-1 odds are only the beginning, even when the fly rod expert is considered to have the highest level of skill. These are the men who eventually became Hal Chittum's clients, and he guided some to world records. Now Hal's clients include me with a fly rod tarpon record of 82½ pounds on 6-pound-class leader tippet and a 107½-pounder using a bait-casting outfit, with a Texas rigged plastic worm on 6-pound-class line. Others include Lenny Berg with a 128-pound tarpon on 10-pound tippet, Billy Pate with a 155-pound tarpon on 12-pound tippet, and Billy's 182-pound tarpon on 15-pound tippet.

It is the 15-pound record that Marvin Levine is now shooting for. But it is much more than that firing up Hal: It's that 200-pound 'poon, something he has wanted more than any other fish in his life.

For six long hours, Marvin and Hal fight the tarpon. In the shallows, through the channels, up the Chassahowitzka River until, with night falling, Hal gets them close enough for a shot with the 8-foot kill gaff.

But the fish is not through. When the steel strikes, its huge body shakes violently, launching the 225-pound guide as if he were a pole vaulter into the water 8 feet away, the gaff still in his hands. For two minutes, the fish tows him, scraping and bumping along the bottom. Finally, he knows he has to let go or drown. He comes up sputtering, "I'm sorry. I lost the fish."

But he hasn't. The hook holds, and the fish jumps for the first time since they hooked it six hours ago. They see it is indeed the all-time tarpon record on fly. The magnificent body crashes down, and the gaff falls free. They recover it and fight for another 20 minutes before the fish stops in the shallows. Hal stretches out with the gaff. The fish veers as the point plunges into it.

At that instant, the 15-pound tippet parts, and the fish is free.

According to the rules, the fight is over. Stunned, speechless, Chittum withdraws the gaff, with one palm-size scale still impaled on the point.

That was all that remained of what would have been the largest tarpon ever caught on a fly.

Above. This is what is frequently referred to as a gill-rattling jump.

Below. The fly on the outside of the tarpon's jaw suggests the need to bow to the jumping fish. When you bow, even if the fly comes loose—and it often does—there's a good chance it will rehook in another spot as shown here.

chapter 33

Lefty's Short Course on Giant Tarpon

*How my "classroom" on fishing for giant tarpon helped
Lefty Kreh get ready to tackle his first 100-pounder.*

The year was 1966, and I had been back flying airplanes for Pan Am for a little
over two years, after a five-year layoff making my living as a backcountry fishing
guide. I had recently sold my house on Little Torch Key and moved up to the
village of Kendale, a newly developed area in the southwest section of Miami.

Lefty Kreh had recently accepted a position as manager of the Metropolitan
Miami Fishing Tournament, the largest and oldest fishing tournament in the
world. Doing so required him to move from his home state of Maryland to somewhere
in South Florida near Miami. This "somewhere" turned out to be a block-and-a-half
walk from my house in Kendale.

As you can well imagine, when I was not in the cockpit for Pan Am, Lefty and I
spent many hours tying flies, rigging tackle together, and talking about flats-fishing
techniques. I had promised Lefty that I would take him down to my old tarpon
haunts the first time we had a good weather forecast over the prime moon tides in
April. That is when tarpon start showing up in large numbers.

I made sure that we started Lefty's tarpon adventures with a short course on fishing for giant tarpon. The "classroom" was at my house the day before we planned to
fish. I wanted to work with Lefty on the proper knots to tie and the proper way to rig

Facing. Stu and Lefty Kreh lifting Lefty's first big tarpon into *Mom's Worry.*

your equipment. I was very emphatic that no detail could be overlooked, that every piece of equipment used to battle those monsters must be checked, and in first-rate condition.

I explained that the hard or stiff monofilament was what we needed for tippet leader material. It cast better, helping turn over a big fly tied on a 4/0 hook. But more important, it does not nick and cut so easily when the rough scales of the tarpon hit it during the fight. Using what the DuPont Company named a "Stu Apte Improved Blood Knot," I tied the stiff 12-pound to a foot of 100-pound monofilament bite tippet that would be attached to the fly.

Lefty had attached a 6-foot section of 30-pound material to the fly line with a simple nail knot. I stressed the importance of pulling that nail knot down smoothly and firmly and then covering it with three coats of Pliobond, a flexible rubber-base glue. I explained that this coating might not make the joint stronger, but it would allow the knot to feed smoothly through the tip-top and rod guides, without the danger of hanging in a guide when the fish is ready to be landed.

Lefty had previously put 200 yards of 27-pound Dacron on his fly reel. We agreed that Dacron was much better than nylon because it didn't stretch—a decided advantage. He had served a loop in the back end of his fly line, spliced a loop in his backing, and then fed one loop through the other to get a smooth connection.

Our attention was next diverted to the drag adjustment on the reel. We wrapped the leader end around the hook on a scale, and adjusted the drag until it read approximately 4 pounds, pulling directly from the reel. We knew that as the normal curve in the rod developed while fighting a fish, the drag coming from the end of the rod could increase up to 20 percent.

I attached an orange and yellow divided-wing streamer that I tied on a 4/0 stainless hook using six neck hackles, three on each side of the hook, and three neck hackles, two yellow with an orange between them, palmered up the shank of the hook and tied off. The fly was very lightly dressed, measuring only 3 inches long. Lefty thought that it might look too small to interest a huge tarpon. I explained that the streamer had to sink quickly, and a big, fluffy fly won't get down to cruising fish fast enough. The hook point was touched with a file to ensure its sharpness. No detail was missed.

"Well, that does it," Lefty said as I set the rigged fly rod, reel, line, and fly in the corner. "That's a good start for my short course."

Next morning, at what Lefty called an unholy hour of three o'clock, we were on our way driving south from Miami to Little Torch Key, three hours away, where I kept my boat, Mom's Worry. While Lefty was driving, I started explaining to him how to look for tarpon.

Tarpon have a rudimentary lung and can breathe air like humans, so it is important to be looking in the distance for rolling tarpon all the time.

Fortunately, Joe Brooks had explained to both of us some years before how to look for fish underwater. Joe said, "Imagine the surface is a pane of glass; look through it, not at it."

I double-checked with Lefty, making sure that he had polarized sunglasses, a must for being able to see fish under the surface before they saw you.

We were both in high spirits as we drove through the Keys. I had explained to Lefty that this was the time of year when the tarpon came in from the ocean, swimming with the incoming tide through the various channels onto the flats and into the backcountry.

My confidence crashed when we got out fishing. Wind conditions were bad, gusty, and the water that was normally clear was roiled. After a three-hour drive and a blown weather forecast, I was not a happy camper. I knew that under the present conditions, it would require extreme concentration, scanning the bottom in order to see any tarpon. After a while, Lefty said that his eyeballs felt like they were sticking out a foot in front of his face and that his eyes belonged to someone else.

I spotted some fish about 70 feet away, and brought Lefty out of his daze with a hoarse whisper, "Over to the left, seventy feet, nine o'clock. Quick! Cast to them!"

"Where?" Lefty wanted to know.

"Dammit, quick, cast where I'm pointing!" I yelled as I pointed with the pushpole.

Lefty made a false cast and shot the heavy streamer 70 feet in the direction I'd pointed. The wind was now blowing 15 knots and caught the fly just before it landed, turning the heavy streamer back 3 feet to the left. The fly hit and the bottom blew up as three tremendous black-green fish boiled out of there.

"Imagine the surface is a pane of glass; look through it, not at it."

Lefty told folks later that I groaned in real anguish and commenced to rant at him, sounding somewhat like a preacher at a revival meeting.

Lefty hung his head in despair and said he was looking for a fish adorned in silver, not realizing that under most conditions, the backs of these giant fish could be dark or even blend in with their surroundings.

He nodded as he probably had years ago when scolded by a teacher. Then he turned around, looking back at me, and said, "This short course can be rough on first-time tarpon fishermen."

I poled us across three more flats, finding a few tarpon, but never getting close enough for Lefty to make a cast. The roiled water and the wind made it tough going for both of us.

We had about two hours to kill before the tide would be right again, so Lefty poled me over a large shallow grass flat I had been finding bonefish on during that particular phase of the tide. Suddenly he said, "Hey, Stu! Isn't that a fish at eleven o'clock, sixty feet?"

It was a permit closing fast, coming toward the boat as the boat was going downwind toward the permit. I barely had time to roll the fly out of my fingers, shooting a little of the fly line on my backcast, and drop the bonefish fly 2 feet in front of its face. I had to immediately start stripping line in order to work the fly because of our rapid closure. My heart was in my mouth as this hefty permit followed the fly right up to the boat before it swirled away. I turned to face Lefty and said, "I have cast to hundreds of them, and have yet to get one to take a fly."

"Cast up current, to the head of the school . . ."

We had been up since two o'clock that morning, the sun was hot, and we were beat. So I shoved the pushpole into the soft bottom, harnessing the boat to it with a dock line. We stretched out on the boat seats and took a nap. Lefty awoke first and caught a couple of small sharks on a fly while looking around for a rolling tarpon.

I woke up to the crashing sound of a school of mullet being scattered by a school of feeding tarpon.

"Get your rod!" I said as I struggled to pull the pushpole out of the bottom. These tarpon had cornered a school of mullet in the bend of a 10-foot-deep channel about 200 feet up the bank from our nap site. When I cut the distance to around 100 feet, I pointed with the pushpole and said, "Do you see that big green patch over there?"

"You mean that green bottom?"

"That's not bottom, that's a bunch of big tarpon. I'm going to pole you a little closer. Get ready."

Lefty watched intently as I silently moved him closer. "Let me know when you can start to pick out individual shapes of fish," I said.

"My God, they are tarpon!" yelled Lefty.

"Cast upcurrent, to the head of the school—hurry, they're starting to slowly move away."

Lefty drove the 4/0 fly 80 feet, allowing for the left-hand crosswind, letting it fall 12 feet in front of the fish, which were slowly moving into the current toward his fly as it sank to their depth.

I was holding my breath as Lefty began foot-long slow strips, moving the fly with the current. He had the rod butt nestled in his belly. I could see the fly pass two giant fish, both more than 6 feet long. The fly went by one giant fish after another, until it seemed as though it had passed through the whole school.

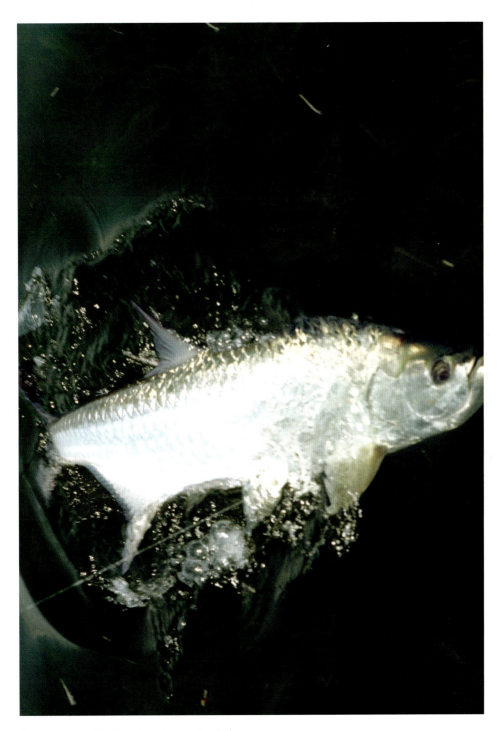

A tarpon when it is almost ready to be landed.

I was starting to get that sick feeling in the pit of my stomach when I noticed a long black shape swing away from the school and start angling toward the fly, slowly catching up to it. It seemed like the fly was only 15 feet from the boat when the tarpon moved up with a swish of its tail, opened its bucket-size mouth, and sucked the fly down. Lefty waited for the mouth to close, and as the fish made an ever-so-slight turn away, he struck repeatedly, deeply embedding the hook.

All hell broke loose. The fish leaped straight up, more than 5 feet out of the water, showering us both with spray. I was hoping that despite this intense excitement, Lefty would remember some of the things we'd talked about the night before, like, "Forget the fish, make sure the line feeds smoothly through the guides."

I let out a sigh of relief when the line came tight against the reel. The fish made two wild greyhounding jumps going directly away from us, screaming 75 yards of backing off the reel. Lefty did a magnificent job of bowing by extending his arm and the rod toward this monster-like fish. That does help prevent the fish from falling on the line, but most important, it helps soften the shock and strain on your leader created by the sudden separation. I had explained as much to Lefty, telling him that a 100-pound tarpon in the air weighs 100 pounds. The same 100-pound tarpon in the water will probably weigh only 10 or 15 pounds, because of its displacement in the water.

Thirty minutes seemed to fly by, and this magnificent silver king was now that many feet from the boat.

Every time that tarpon swam to the left, Lefty pulled the rod down and to his right. He would do the same thing in reverse, every time it wanted to swim to the right. Each time, I could see the fish yielding a bit more, until it lay gasping at the boat, with Lefty gulping for his share of air, too.

That "Short Course for Giant Tarpon" had paid off with Lefty's first tarpon weighing more than 100 pounds. Now it's 2014 as I write this, and during the 50-odd years that have passed, Lefty has taught tens of thousands of people to become fine fly fishing anglers.

Facing. Stu congratulates Lefty Kreh on a tarpon that topped 100 pounds—Lefty's first big tarpon.

General Norman "Stormin' Norman" Schwarzkopf with his first big tarpon on a fly.

chapter 34

Stormin' Norman's Tarpon Campaign

When General Schwarzkopf lost a big tarpon fishing with me, he told me,
"Stu, I don't like to lose." That's when I told him how to fight the next battle.

Some years ago, I fished with Capt. Sean O'Keefe out of Key West, a guide I'd previously heard good things about. Indeed, I had a great day of shallow-water backcountry sight fishing for big tarpon. I hooked and landed only the smallest one of about 50 or 60 pounds, but had at least 12 opportunities to cast at big fish.

The following December, Sean called to invite me to fish with him again on open dates in April. During that same period, the tournament director of a sailfish event going on at the same time got in touch to say that General Norman Schwarzkopf had asked him to find out if I would be available to take him out fly fishing for tarpon this year. He added that the general needed left-handed fly reels.

"Absolutely, the pleasure would be all mine, and I'll make sure to have left-handed-wind fly reels for him," I eagerly responded.

I got in touch with General Schwarzkopf at a private cocktail party before the tournament, and we formulated a game plan for the next day's tarpon trip. We arranged for a second skiff to include General Ellis, run by Sgt. Robert Allen, the Port Security Director.

All was going according to plan, and Sean had a good plan for starting off the morning not far from the marina, saying there had been many tarpon in the Boca Chica channel on that early morning incoming tide.

Fifteen minutes later, we were idling up to a shallow edge of the channel and we could see three different schools of tarpon rolling farther out, looking like they were coming our way. Shutting off the engine and using his pushpole to hold the boat in position with the bow pointed toward the incoming tide and the tarpon, Sean said, "Looks like they are right on schedule, better get the rod with the intermediate ghost tip out and be ready." A slight northeasterly breeze was coming offshore, giving us a good setup with some protection from the shoreline.

Making a cast to lay out the line needed for the general to cast, I passed the 11-weight fly rod over and backed out of his way. I casually asked him to make a few practice casts to get used to the rod.

It was immediately obvious that this was the first time he'd ever had a fly rod that big in his hand. After a little instruction and half a dozen practice casts, he was able to cast all of the 55 feet of line I had out of the rod tip, it would be more than enough for this type of fishing situation.

Turning to face me, he said, "Stu, thanks for the instruction. You have a good way of presenting what has to be done."

"Thank you, sir," I replied, adding that he wasn't the first four-star I'd had in my boat.

"Oh yeah, who else?" he asked, looking directly at me.

"Well, sir, back in 1960 when I was laid off from Pan Am making a full-time living as a backcountry guide here in the Florida Keys, I guided General Cates, the ex-Commandant of the Marine Corps during the Korean War, for three days of bonefishing."

"Humph, only a marine general," he said with a twinkle in his eyes and a chuckle.

All this time, I could see the schools of tarpon getting closer. Then, as if by magic, two slow-rolled, coming up from the deep part of the channel angling toward us.

"Hurry, General!" I said in a somewhat hushed voice. "Drop the fly right at eleven o'clock." My voice continued as the tarpon came on. "Good . . . let it sink for a moment . . . now, strip in some line to get the slack out. That was okay—now, pick up and cast right back to the same place; I think they're still lying out there."

He cast again, and my advice continued, "Perfect . . . start a slow strip . . . twitch the line at the end of each strip." The words were barely out of my mouth when I saw his fly line stop. "I think he's got it!" I whispered. "Hurry, strip the slack out and set the hook."

No sooner said than done, the next sound we all heard was the fly line, then the backing screaming from the general's reel and 50 yards out a 75-pound silver king came out in a flashy, high-flying jump. Almost as quickly, Sean had his engine trimmed all the way down and started, pulled his pushpole out of the bottom, put the boat in forward gear, seemingly all in one motion, and turned the steering wheel directly toward the fish. Now 150 yards out, this feisty tarpon was once again jumping.

Standing slightly behind and on the left side of General Schwarzkopf, I suggested he lift as much line out of the water as he could, winding line quickly while Sean moved the boat toward his fish.

The general appeared to be having somewhat of a problem cranking the reel with his left hand, but in all fairness, he did manage to pick up line as we got closer to that young adult tarpon. About 20 minutes into the fight, we were within 30 feet of Mr. 'Poon, when for some reason not known to either the general or me, instead of winding the reel handle forward, he wound in the opposite direction, creating a serious amount of slack line within the reel. Of course, the tarpon chose just that moment to surge and start another short run, creating a backlash in the reel, breaking the 20-pound-test tippet with the surge.

"Close, but no cigar, General," I laughingly said.

"Sure, close only works with horseshoes and hand grenades," he replied while flexing his arms. His face stern, he said, "Stu, I don't like what you have done to me . . . don't like to lose."

"This was just the first battle, sir, not the war," I replied.

While Sean was running his boat the half a mile we had traveled fighting the fish back to the edge of the channel, I was already stripping fly line off Sean's left-hand-wind reel in order to wind it back onto my right-hand-wind reel. If the good general was going to fight another tarpon, I wanted him to wind with what I now knew was his dominant right hand. By the time we were back in position, I had selected a new leader with the same type fly from my leader stretcher case, and was tying it onto the butt section of the leader coming from the fly line. One thing I had learned a long time ago about fly fishing for tarpon is you have to be ready, or you'll miss some good opportunities.

"This was just the first battle, sir, not the war,"

As I was stripping fly line off the reel to get the general set up, I heard a big splash, and both Sean and the general asked if I'd seen that one jump.

"No, I was too busy getting things set up," I said, looking up and seeing three fish roll just out of our 55-foot range. Quickly stripping more line off the reel, I roll-cast the fly out of my fingers forward, then shooting line on the backcast and laying out 75 feet of line. After letting it sink for the count of four, I started my normal easy tarpon strip, with a twitch on the end of each strip, when the line came tight in midstrip. Setting the hook smartly, I quickly turned to the general, pushing the rod into his hands and saying, "Take it, this is really your fish."

Sean had everything secured with the engine running in less than 30 seconds—on her first jump, we could see she was a full-blown adult of more than 100 pounds. This time I got my left-hand cotton fish fighting glove out of my case and waited for the right moment when the fish was not screaming line or coming toward us to put it onto the general's left hand.

I now knew I'd made a wise decision, having General Schwarzkopf fight the fish with a right-hand-retrieving fly reel. He was winding three times faster with his right hand than he had on the other fish using his left hand.

Getting a better look at that handsome fish on its next two jumps, I now estimated its weight at 120 pounds. A true adult, for sure . . .

One hour and 40 minutes into the fight after, a tour of two different marinas, the mooring harborage of two dozen sailboats, into a shallow mangrove-lined bay, General Schwarzkopf had the leader's nail knot in through the tip-top of the fly rod, which was the criterion in all release tournaments that signified a caught fish.

I could tell the general's back was creating an enormous amount of pain, on top of the muscle and stomach pain he was feeling from a long hard fight with a tremendous fish. I've always said that I never caught a big fish using light tackle without hurting during the fight and again the following day.

Mission accomplished, I thought, *let's not have a successful operation and have the patient die.* Reaching around with my right hand, I gently but firmly took the fly rod out of the general's hands.

"Damn good job, sir, on one helluva big 'poon," I said.

Sean was patting him on the shoulder with congratulations, too. That evening at the sailfish tournament party, three of us—my wife, Jeannine; Sean; and I—were invited to sit at the general's table for dinner. And as you could well imagine, much of the conversation had to do with fly fishing for tarpon and looking forward to the next time.

This 200-pound plus tarpon managed to throw the fly on this, its first jump.

When a triple-digit tarpon is brought boatside, the fight may not be over.
It can quickly explode into a jump right into your face.

chapter 35

Taming the Triple

Battling and releasing a three-digit tarpon is a goal many serious fly fishers dream about. Here's my best advice on how to make it happen, and what to expect when your big chance comes.

Fishing has always been the greatest thing in my life. In fact, it is my life, because I am a professional fisherman. In that fishing life, nothing has ever made me happier than when I have a fly rod in hand and I'm prospecting the Florida Keys flats for tarpon.

Developing new and better tackle is another special interest of mine. Luckily, I was born in Miami, where excellent fishing was always nearby. It has also been an area where light-tackle fishing for big fish has produced a whole new cult of outdoorsmen.

The light-tackle bug bit me at the tender age of 12, when I acquired an old split-bamboo casting rod and a Shakespeare Superior freshwater plug-casting reel. With that rig I landed my first tarpon, a 15-pounder. A few years later, I earned enough money for my first fly rod, and I was hooked for keeps.

Homer Rhode Jr., then a game warden and noted fly fisherman, taught me how to tie saltwater flies, and in 1949, I caught my first tarpon on one. A year later, I landed my first really big tarpon, a 96½ pounder, but it was taken on a plug near Marco Island. It seemed as if I always had a fishing rod of some kind in my hands in those days. Now let's advance the clock. . . .

The month was April. The year was 1962 and I was a fishing guide in the Florida Keys. My customer was Ray Donnersberger of Highland Park, Illinois, and for the past hour he had been hooked to a tarpon we both wanted badly. I knew that fish would be a contender for the all-time fly rod record in the Metropolitan Miami Fishing Tournament.

Ray was fishing with a new-type glass fly rod, and this was definitely not the time for experimenting. I knew of no man I would rather have had in my boat fighting that fish. Ray was 6 feet 4 inches tall and weighed only about 180 pounds, but he moved like a cat and battled fish as if his life depended upon it. He was a top-notch fly caster, a fantastic person, and a great conservationist. I wasn't really worried about losing that tarpon.

The day had been flat calm when we neared Loggerhead Bank and spotted the first school of about 30 tarpon circling on the surface. As I pulled near the school, Ray presented his fly to a large fish. He made his cast just to the outside of the circle so that on the retrieve his fly would move in the same direction as the fish in order not to alarm them. The tarpon had taken the fly eagerly, but too much floating grass and seaweed getting on the fly line made the fight a difficult one. Finally the moment of truth was at hand.

When it comes time to land a big tarpon, it is important that you have a rod with sufficient butt strength to lift its head to the surface. I was ready with the gaff, and Ray was working the fish into position. Just as I made my move, Ray exerted a bit more pressure than that Fenwick thin-walled rod had to offer, and it literally exploded into six pieces just as I struck the tarpon. I had gaffed that fish at the same instant the rod came apart!

The Met Tournament rules stated that a broken rod disqualified the catch. Did the rod break before or after the fish had been legally caught? Ray, being the sportsman that he was, refused to claim the fish even though it weighed 128 pounds—three pounds heavier than the Met record at that time.

Now let's shift the scene to another April, eight years later—April 10, 1970, to be exact. I'm no longer the guide. The guide is now Capt. Bob Montgomery of Key West. I am the angler, and Frank Moss of New York is with me in the boat. Frank was then the editor-in-chief of *Sport Fishing* magazine. The object of our fishing quest was the same: to catch a tarpon big enough to be a Met Tournament fly rod record.

Facing. You often hear the expression "jumping a tarpon." You may not land a single tarpon by the end of the day, but if you say "we jumped three fish," people will understand what you mean.

The tarpon were there, all right, and I jumped my first fish of the day, about a 75-pounder. I was using a 9½-foot experimental Pflueger Supreme glass fly rod. Can you believe it? They say some folks never learn.

That 75-pound tarpon was active. I got five fast jumps out of him before he liberated himself about 50 feet from the skiff by throwing the fly.

I rapidly changed leaders, tied on a new fly, and was just pulling the knot tight when I looked up to see a school of tarpon within casting distance. A very large fish was in the lead. Nervously I stripped line from the reel, false cast one time, and made my presentation. The huge tarpon took the fly as if it were sugar candy, and the moment she felt the hook, she jumped.

I was awed as I watched it come out of the water. This was the fish I had been seeking all my life—the fabled fly rod tarpon that would go over 200 pounds. But I tried to keep calm and settle down for the struggle ahead.

One hour and four jumps later, after having had that fish boatside for gaffing one time, I watched with a sick, sinking sensation as my fly finally pulled out and my trophy swam away unscathed.

I sat down, exhausted, and rerigged my leader with shaking hands.

Captain Montgomery cranked the engine, and we ran back to where we had hooked that fish. He poled no more than 200 yards before I could see another school coming down the bank. Again, this school held an extremely large specimen. Perhaps as large as the one I had just lost. I presented my fly to her, but as happens sometimes, a smaller fish beat her to it, and I found myself hooked to the wrong fish.

"Only a lousy hundred-pounder," I remarked somewhat ridiculously, as there was a tremendous difference in size from the previous tarpon. And I had my heart set on something bigger.

After the first 15 minutes of the fight, I heard an ominous creaking and cracking coming from the butt section of the experimental fly rod I was using. I continued to pressure the fish, which was looking bigger all the time.

The tarpon made its fifth jump, and just as I was bowing to her—to my utter amazement—the bottom half of the rod handle with the reel seat and reel simply dropped off and landed in the bottom of the boat. (I later learned from the manufacturer that this rod had been designed for casting experiments only and the handle had been held in place with mere glue.)

Facing. The jump is one of the most beautiful and exciting moments in fishing. It's also the same moment the fish may throw the hook.

Fortunately, I never have more than 2 to 2½ pounds of drag on the reel, and I apply most of the pressure to the fish with my hands on the line. That gave me a chance to scramble around the bottom of the boat for the reel. It was just like trying to catch a live snake as the tarpon peeled off line.

For the last six or seven minutes of the fight, I played the fish with the unattached reel seat and reel tucked under the end of the rod. In this way, I was able to work the fish within easy gaffing range—though gaffing one of those tough-scaled giants is never a sure thing. Back at the dock, the fish weighed 151 pounds 4 ounces and exceeded the fly rod world record (which I held) by exactly 4 ounces. But, almost more important to me, that fish would've been a new Metropolitan Miami Tournament record. I suppose I could have used the rationality that the rod did not actually break, that it had merely come unglued, but I felt I had to disqualify the catch in the interest of good sportsmanship.

Even so, that tarpon did bring a prize—the 1970 Philip Wylie Tough Luck Trophy, which the Met Tournament awards each year to the angler having the worst "break."

I think it's worth mentioning here that the very next day with virtually the same tides and other favorable conditions, we fished hard in the same locations without ever seeing a single tarpon.

That's tarpon fishing! That's also the reason it's so important to be all set for action when the fish do show. I have fished countless days for tarpon with nary a cast to one. On the other hand, I have had quite a number of days that I've landed as many as seven big tarpon in a day.

"...keeping good notes on moon phases, time of the tides in each spot that you encounter them..."

To have your best chance at catching the triple-digit tarpon, you will have to pay—one way or the other. Pay your dues by spending countless days of hunting these critters. By keeping good notes on moon phases, time of the tides in each spot that you encounter them, studying their habits in general. The wisdom gained by those efforts is not something that develops quickly.

Or pay by hiring a good guide who has been studying tarpon for years. That is my recommendation.

But if you have the time and the inclination to take up the challenge on your own, the following information should help.

I have caught many 100-pound-plus tarpon on a fly during every month of the year. That being said, it seems tarpon come onto the flats best when the water temperature ranges between 72 and 88 degrees, depending on the season. Also of help is a big push of water that you would get from either the new moon or the full moon tides, and light- or no-wind conditions.

All those factors are very important, and if you live in the Florida Keys, you can pick the days when all of them come together. But if you have only a few days or even weeks to come to the Florida Keys for tarpon—everything else being equal, such as wind, tides, and so on—the best months should be April, May, and June.

If you do come to the Florida Keys during the winter months, and happen to have the proper conditions for tarpon to be on the flats, try to select a flat for fishing late in the afternoon. The warmer, late-afternoon water on a number of flats can pull fish from nearby channels. Knowing which flats reliably pull fish on winter afternoons of warmer water can make you a busy angler or a busy guide, as the case may be.

In fact, if you are down in the Florida Keys during the summer months of July, August, September, then cooler water will be your friend and the best fishing will be from daylight until about 10:30 in the morning, and again the last couple of hours before sundown.

Unless you have a past track record on which fly to use in each area, a good rule of thumb to follow is to use a lighter colored fly over light bottom or clear water. Use darker patterns over dark grass or discolored water or both.

The type of fly tackle and how it is rigged are critical in catching a big tarpon. Without experience, you're far better off using your guide's tackle. Depending on the angler's ability, a 10-, 11-, or 12-weight fly rod will do the job. Unlike the old days, there is a multitude of good rods on the market today. I have personally been using a 9-foot Diamondback Saltwater model rod. It is a great casting tool, and a super fish-fighting weapon.

In the past eight or ten years, there have been more new fly reels introduced to the marketplace than for all the previous years. It is important to purchase a good bar stock aluminum fly reel. They are expensive, $400 to $800 each. With proper care, these reels will last more than a lifetime, and can become heirlooms to be passed on for generations. I have either been using the new Tibor fly reel, since Ted Juracsik, with the help of Lefty Kreh and Flip Pallot, designed and started manufacturing it, or the STH BT&T, a reel, manufactured in Argentina.

I am often asked what fly line I use for tarpon. The answer is easy. If I were to purchase only one line, it would be the multitip fly line. With it, I know I can cover any fishing situation that may arise.

I am able to change from a floating tip to a mono-type intermediate tip, a medium sinking tip, or a fast sinking tip. I can make that change in less time than it would require me to take a different rod from the rod rack and strip the line off the reel. No matter what brand or type of line you do use, I recommend that you stay with the line weight that the rod manufacturer suggests.

There are a number of new products on the market that some anglers are using for backing—Magibraid Dacron, Spiderwire, or Spectra to name a few. For the most part, I stick with the old standby I have used for about 40 years, Gudebrod Dacron.

The correct method of connecting the backing to the fly line is very important. Tie a Bimini twist, forming a loop approximately 10 inches long with the backing. If my fly line is new, I will cut it back to approximately 85 feet long. Then I strip approximately ¼ inch of finish off the line, double the line over, forming a loop approximately ¾ inch long. I tie a nail knot over the bottom part of the loop, using 10-pound-test monofilament, then tie a second nail knot as close to the first one as I can. I then trim all the ends and put a couple of coatings of Pliobond over the two nail knots. I have the backing on the fly reel with the Bimini twist available, and pass the backing through the small loop on the fly line, then open the large loop in the backing and pass the fly reel through it. When you snug this loop-to-loop connection, make sure they come together like a figure eight.

I cannot stress enough the importance of being properly rigged and ready when big tarpon are your quarry. How many shots will you get? For sure, not enough to squander. You'll want to make every one count.

Out on the water, when you see a bunch of tarpon, don't "flock shoot" the school. Try to stay calm enough to pick an individual big fish to cast to. Be aware that the smaller fish often are more aggressive than the bigger ones. Don't look right at the fish you're casting to; look at the spot you want your fly to land in, while watching the fish with your peripheral vision.

When you do hook that monster tarpon, somewhere close to 150 pounds, it is paramount that you use the proper fish-fighting techniques in order to land it quickly. I know of some long fights where big tarpon were fought for 12 and 14 hours before losing them. During one of those extended fights, the boat finally ran out of gas and the fish kept right on going. I know both the angler and guide.

Experience has taught me over and over that big tarpon—big fish of virtually all types—should be fought fast and hard. (See chapter 28 for a discussion of big-fish fighting tips.)

If you go for your triple-digit silver king and end up fighting it hour after hour, down channels, past bridges, even out to sea, your fight is not likely to have a happy ending.

Now, go prove me wrong!

Facing. Sometimes it seems to take forever to hook-up on a big tarpon.
But once on, the fish might be gone in one jump. With the line slack,
you're flooded with a mixture of excitement and disappointment.

Ian Davis of Yellow Dog Fly Fishing Adventures, shows the proper way to handle a bonefish when it is being released. *Photo by Ian Davis.*

chapter 36

Today's Catch, Tomorrow's Dreams

Catch-and-release is an angling code that makes a lot of sense. These rules help make the ethic work.

For all anglers and captains, the moment of truth comes when the fish is at hand, in the net, in the boat, in the shallows. Now what?

W hen you're after fish you covet for great meals, they're going into the cooler as long as you haven't exceeded the limit. No ifs, ands, or buts about it. They're going home with you.

But what if you've landed a fish you know you don't want to keep to eat? No problem, you're going to release it.

But what if it's a prize catch—a personal best or coveted trophy? That's a question that rates some thought.

One option, and a good one, is to take a photograph of that trophy catch, and then release your fish in good condition. Then you will still have your trophy, in the photograph, and the fish will live to fight again someday. That's truly a win–win situation, the catch-and-release code of many anglers today.

In the introduction to Lee Wulff's *Handbook of Freshwater Fishing,* published by Lippincott in 1939, the renowned Atlantic salmon fly fisherman probably said it best when he wrote, "Game fish are too valuable to be caught only once." A number of years ago the Fly Fishing Federation (FFF) made a statement on its logo promoting catch-and-release. "Limit your kill; don't kill your limit!"

A young Capt. Hal Chittum goes into
the water to revive a tired tarpon.

Ron Taylor, from the Florida Marine Research Institute wrote, "Fishing effort in Florida has increased dramatically over the past decade and is forecast to continue as Florida's resident population of 14.7 million increases daily by about 1,000 people. More than 40 million tourists visit the state annually, most with coastal destinations." That necessitates the state setting minimum and maximum sizes, "slot" limits, to create a trophy fishery.

The fate of fish caught by hook-and-line and released largely depends on the expertise and dexterity of the angler. Anglers practicing these few straightforward and intuitive techniques can increase survival of the released fishes.

Back in my guiding heyday, the early 1960s when I was on the water for hire more than 330 days a year, I would never *knowingly* kill a fish to take a photograph for a client. But I did run my guiding businesses as a business, promoting the mounting of many species of fish, especially tarpon, bonefish, and permit.

Those were the years before the taxidermists were doing fiberglass mounts, and they had to use the actual skin, which made it necessary to kill the fish. As the captain, I received a 30 or 40 percent commission from the taxidermists, and I am not proud to tell you that Pflueger Taxidermy said I provided more mounts during those years than any other three top backcountry guides combined.

I have always considered myself a sportsman and a conservationist, striving to do what I thought was best for the ecology. Up until recently, I thought lip gaffing—putting a release gaff through the soft membrane of the tarpon's lower jaw in order to hold it up for a picture—would not permanently damage the fish. Recent studies by various marine laboratories have come out with a series of guidelines to follow that will help the survival rate of all caught-and-released fish.

As one of the founding fathers and a member of the executive board of Bonefish Tarpon Trust (BTT), I sit in on many meetings with marine biologists from various universities and marine laboratories. I would like to pass on some general tips for proper catch-and-release from Dr. Aaron Adams, fisheries biologist at Mote Marine Laboratory (BTT's Director of Operations):

- **Tackle:** Use tackle and fish-fighting techniques that will help land the fish quickly. The fishing equipment and line strength used should ensure that the fish can be landed in a reasonable length of time and not played out until it is completely exhausted.

- **Bait, Lures, and Hooks:** Whenever possible, use steel or bronze hooks. They are less toxic than cadmium-coated hooks and dissolve faster than stainless steel hooks. Use pliers to pinch down the barbs on your lures and flies. This precaution reduces the amount of handling time.

Studies on striped bass, spotted sea trout, redfish, and snook have shown that live bait was used in most cases of hook-related mortality and that "gut hooking" was the primary cause of death.

If using live or dead baits, use circle hooks, which are designed to hook the fish in its jaw, greatly reducing the risk of deep-hooking a fish, a major cause of fish mortality. Remember, when using a circle hook, it is not necessary to set the hook when you feel the fish take the bait. Just start reeling when you feel the pressure, and the hook will set itself.

- **Fish Handling:** How the fish is handled can have huge effects on its survival. Of course, the best approach is never to remove the fish from the water while removing the hook. If the fish doesn't swim off on its own, it may need some recovery time. Gently hold it under its chin and base of the tail until it regains the wherewithal to swim off. If there are sharks present, some recovery time in the live well may be beneficial.

  If it is necessary to remove the fish from the water, be sure to wet your hands first. This extra step reduces the amount of slime removed from the fish—slime that is an important barrier against infection. Never use a towel to hold the fish, even a wet one!

  Although it is tempting, don't lift a large fish by the lower jaw. The weight of the fish hanging from the lower jaw can tear ligaments in the narrow stretch of flesh between the underside of its gills, making it difficult for the fish to feed and also may stretch its spine, which could cause death within a few days.

  Do not put fingers inside the gill cover or eye sockets of a fish. A grip device, such as the Boga-Grip, may be used if the body of the fish is supported at all times when lifting to release the fish.

- **Fish Caught in Deep Water:** These individuals may require special handling to promote their survival. When a fish is rapidly brought to the surface from depths of around 30 feet or more, the gases in its swim bladder may have expanded significantly, causing its stomach to be pushed out of its mouth. Venting the air in the swim bladder by making a small insertion with a fine hollow needle or ice pick will increase the fish's survival rate.

- **Photographing Your Catch:** With the availability of digital cameras, we are taking a lot more photographs of our catches. A common mistake is to take the fish out of the water, then get the camera ready, then take the picture.

  It's best to keep the fish in the water until you're fishing partner has the camera ready, you have your equipment where you want it, and you have decided where everyone in the picture will be. Now, most important, when holding the fish, it should be supported with wet hands under its jaw and anal fin.

Controlled studies have shown that most fish carefully released after hook-and-line capture survive. Researchers working in Boca Grande Pass tagged 27 tarpon with sonic transmitters and found that 26 of these hook-and-line-caught fish survived. The only fish that died had been lifted from the water for a prereleased photograph.

Remember: Gently does it when releasing your catch.

Actor and director Paul Michael Glaser watches the late José Wejebe, famous for his long-running *Spanish Fly* TV show, release a nice permit.

There's nothing like leaping tarpon to make your birthday one you'll never forget.

chapter 37

The Birthday Fish

Whenever I think of my birthdays, this is the one that
always comes to mind first. And it always will!

It's May 11, 1982, and my good friend Capt. Ralph Delph of Key West and I decide to celebrate my birthday fly fishing for the Big Momoo—the 200-pound
tarpon at Homosassa, Florida. Just to sweeten the pot, a new TV film producer
has heard about the five days we're going to spend searching for big tarpon.
He asks if he could follow along in a second boat, staying out of our way but
shooting whatever happens.

The plan involves having the producer and his cameraman meet Ralph and me
for dinner on May 10 at the Riverside Villas, right on the Homosassa River. But
the camera crew experiences difficulties renting some of the sound equipment they
need and can't join us until May 13. They will miss the first two days of fishing.

You can probably guess what happens.

The morning starts off in a normal way, with the two of us taking turns. I lead off
by catching a pretty nice fish about 110 pounds; then Ralph nails one that looked to
be around 130 pounds. At that point a nonfishing boat runs right down the center
of tarpon Mecca, forcing us to clench our jaws and fists in anger. That prompts me
to suggest we get away from the boats and run north for about five miles to another
area I know.

We shut down the big engine and start using the electric trolling motors and
pushpole to maneuver us into the proper depth of water where tarpon should be
coming through.

One of the "big ones" we caught and released on my most memorable birthday.

Capt. Ralph Delph's carefully releasing one of the big "poon" we landed.

Ralph sees a fish roll around 300 yards away, and we head toward it. Seventy-five yards off to my right at three o'clock, a school rolls and goes into a daisy chain. A daisy chain involves a doughnut-shaped school of tarpon either mating or trying to ball up baitfish, which go into a circling maneuver when frightened by predators.

It's amazing when you're fishing in 6 to 8 feet of water, and fish aren't rolling but are circling in a daisy chain, how close you can be to them without them knowing you're there.

Ralph poles me to the daisy chain, and we see a very big female in the center of the doughnut. Females are the prizes when loaded with roe because they can weigh an extra 30 pounds or more.

I must cast perfectly in order to get the fly across the other tarpon in the daisy chain. Using a 12-foot leader, most often I can put the leader across some fish without disturbing them. This time my cast is pinpoint perfect, and as I strip the fly in front of the big female, another smaller tarpon makes a quick move, taking the fly. I guess its weight at about 140 pounds. That's not the one that I want, so I try not to come tight. I don't want to set the hook. The fish comes out with a little head-shake and gets rid of the fly. That's just enough commotion to break up the daisy chain, and the school slowly swims away.

Luck stays with us, and in about 100 yards, they stop and chain up again. Ralph once again uses the electrics and the pushpole and maneuvers me into position for a second try at "Madam Big."

The positioning and my cast go as they did the first time. The difference now is that she's not about to let some upstart 140-pounder take that goody away from her.

I'll never forget that jump when I set the hook. She blasts out of the water like a Polaris missile. Fully 8 feet long with a big, thick body. We know that this is a monster, the quintessential legend of Homosassa.

All hell breaks loose in the boat. Ralph stows the pushpole and begins to lower the big outboard. Normally we'd never crank the outboard with another boat nearby, but we knew this to be an exceptional fish and she's screaming line off my reel like there's no tomorrow. Already, 200 yards melts off the reel. Only one other boat is nearby with my friend Capt. Steve Huff, another outstanding Florida Keys guide in Homosassa for the same reasons we were. Ralph radios him and tells him we've got the big one on the line, the fish we've always talked about and imagined catching. Steve immediately says not to worry, and to go ahead and fire up the engine.

This fish quickly develops a constant rhythm with its tail, and doesn't even seem to be exerting a lot of energy. Ralph manages to keep me within 30 to 40 feet of this big lady, allowing me to put maximum pressure on her all the time. During the first 20 minutes of the fight, she rolls periodically, gulping oxygen before heading back toward the bottom. Each time she starts elevating, I put about 2 feet of my fly rod into the water, making her work hard to come to the surface for air.

Notice the IGFA regulation leader with 11-⅞ inches of bite tippet to the fly.

Fifteen minutes of that, and she's set up a rhythm in her rolling. Now I'm beginning to predict when she's coming up for air. My theory of sticking the rod tip underwater and pulling down and back toward her tail is what I nicknamed "down and dirty." This technique makes it difficult for her to get the oxygen, and begins to take its toll. I want this fish to feel that she has to fight her way to the top—a bit of psychology that generally pays off handsomely.

Forty-five minutes into the fight, the nail knot reaches the rod tip and slides past the first stripping guide as the fish nears the boat. I tell Ralph that the next time she comes up, I'll hold her there and he can hit her with the gaff. He moves from the console and gets in front of me in the cockpit. I pressure the fish and it wallows like a drunken sailor.

Ralph braces his knees on the gunwale and sinks the gaff home. In a split second I glimpse a view of the bottom of Ralph's shoes as he's launched over the gunwale into the water beside the fish, having gaffed it just in front of the dorsal fin. He hands the gaff handle to me and starts climbing back into the boat when the gaff comes out of the tarpon's back.

Miraculously, I still have the fish hooked and the fight is on again. Fifteen minutes later, we get the giant tarpon and boat together once more, programmed the same way. This time, however, I ask Ralph to please use my large barbed gaff that I made especially for great big tarpon like this one and not his smaller gaff, which I firmly believed didn't possess a big enough bite in the hook. Ralph, being Ralph, elects to ignore my plea and instead use his smaller gaff yet again.

It's the same scenario all over again, except this time when Ralph strikes the fish with his gaff, it jerks his butt clean out of the boat again, but now it charges more than 50 yards away with Ralph hanging on like a hitchhiker. I don't realize it at the time, but the boat is still in slow-idle forward gear.

This has become no laughing matter. Ralph appears to be in trouble while literally wrestling with a beast far bigger than he—and in its element. Both of Ralph's arms and legs wrap around her. (Later he tells me that he tried to put one hand and arm up through its gill plate in order to secure it while at the same time trying to hold that little gaff hook in place.)

At one point, this monster fish comes up half out of the water with a head-shaking jump, and damned if Ralph isn't still wrapped around it. I drop the fly rod and dash back to the console, quickly advancing the throttle while at the same time swinging the bow toward friend and fish. We're in 8 feet of water and Ralph definitely looks like he's not having fun.

I grab a very large release gaff as the boat approaches the pair. Ralph's console is different from mine, and I somewhat fumble with the controls as I approach them. At what I figure is the right moment, I put his engine in reverse to stop the boat's forward motion, and back into neutral. I charge to the bow, aiming to hook that big tarpon under its lower jaw with my release gaff.

I immediately realize that the boat isn't in neutral, but instead is still in gear and idling forward. I run back to the console, throw the boat in hard reverse, and switch the ignition key off.

Too little and too late! I've got Ralph bore-sighted, and he has to take one arm off the tarpon to keep the stem of the boat from running over him, a move that rolls both him and the fish under, forcing him to release his grip.

The legend of Homosassa gets off the gaff and swims away.

Disappointment. Utter disappointment. And I'm upset at Ralph being stubborn in not using my gaff either time.

Ralph climbs into the boat dejectedly. "Why did you run me over?" he asks.

I explain that I thought he was in serious trouble and, not being familiar with his throttle quadrant, believed we were in neutral rather than idle forward.

Ralph is so full of tarpon slime from being wrapped around that big 'poon that he got everything in the boat coated in that heavy, grease-like film. Actually, the ignominious leavings of that tarpon have put an exclamation mark on the gloom we felt at the moment.

Yes, we fish some more and catch two tarpon that day, and as the hours tick on, Ralph smells like a very ripe tarpon—and I treasure the moments when he stands downwind of me.

We do not mention that big fish even once during the rest of the day or that night in the motel or, for that matter, the next day out fishing. But the next evening at dinner, Ralph turns to me and asks, "What do you think that fish really weighed, Stu?"

I say, "Ralph, let's not influence each other as to the weight." I tear a paper napkin in two, hand him half, and ask him to write down how much he thinks the fish weighed while I do the same.

Ralph jots down "230+" and from my side of the table I write "230 plus." At that time, the largest tarpon ever landed weighed 188 pounds on 16-pound tippet, so this fish even on 12-pound-class tippet would have smashed it. Another irony: Fate has dealt an unfortunate hand to that camera crew, which otherwise would have captured that epic battle on film.

Nineteen years later to the day, May 11, 2001, my young friend Jimmy Holland caught the first 200-pound tarpon on a fly ever. It weighed 202½ pounds and became the International Game Fish Association's 20-pound-class tippet world record. Of course, we can talk "maybes" until the cows fly home, but that gargantuan 'poon that Ralph and I lost would probably have set an unbeatable benchmark.

Facing. Stu's 164-pound birthday tarpon, with Capt. Ralph Delph. The fish was the second fly-rod world record of the day using 12-pound-class tippet.

chapter 38

Those Elusive "Good Old Days"

I've enjoyed mine down to the last turn of
my reel handle. Don't let yours get away!

One advantage of being an old dude (I'm 84 as I write this) is that I can reflect on "the good old days."

For me, that's a lot of "reflecting," because I've more than had my share of good ones.

I was talking about some of those days a few years back while addressing a group of fly fishers. In the Q&A session, one young angler spoke up and said that he didn't know how the fishing was back in the 1950s or '60s, but as far as he was concerned, the fishing was great right then.

I really liked the direction of his thinking. It took me only a nanosecond to answer with, "You're right! These are 'the good old days' of tomorrow!"

You may have been out fishing today, or yesterday, and drew a blank. They just weren't around, or they just weren't hitting. Don't let that throw you. Keep going out, and your great days will come as sure as the turning of the earth. Years from now, you and others will be looking back on the fishing we have right now as "the good old days."

I'm a Florida boy who came along in years that could be described in Charles Dickens's language as "the best of times, the worst of times." I was born in Miami on May 11, 1930, when the country was locked in a depression. By the end of the '30s, World War II was on the horizon. The "best" part of those times was the fishing. I was

Facing. Photo by Pat Ford.

an avid fisherman from almost the time I could first walk. And my homeland Florida offered everything I could possibly want to pursue with hook and line.

Even my birthday seems to have been destined to be connected to Florida's best fishing. For whatever it's worth, the fact is that more record tarpon have been caught on my May 11 birthday than on any other day. As Casey Stengel used to love saying, "You could look it up."

A key point in my development as an angler occurred in 1946, the year after the war had ended, when at age 16, I first had a fly rod in my hand. My line was an 8-weight, weight-forward, Cortland GBF Torpedo Head. What a great name that was for this young lad. Torpedo Head! How could I fail with an angling weapon like that?

Because I have been fishing for more than 60 years in South Florida waters, I am often asked, What major changes have I seen in the fishery?

Back in the mid-1950s through 1964, when I was laid off from Pan Am and made my living as a backcountry guide in the Lower Florida Keys, I began keeping a daily fishing log. It covered where I found the tarpon, permit, and bonefish; what the air and water temperatures were like, the winds, the tides, in each of the areas I fished.

Today, I can check those logs, match the conditions to the present, and head out to the flats with high expectations for success.

Will the fishing be like those "good old days"?

No, it will not. There are well-documented problems with bonefish right now in the Keys, with better days hopefully coming in the future. The tarpon fishing is not the same as it was 40 years ago either. It's still damn good, though, and I'm going after them every chance I get.

The tarpon fishing has changed since I first started fishing the Florida Keys. I remember seeing many schools of tarpon with 80 to 150 fish in a school, swimming down various shallow banks, near the deep channels. They showed up like clockwork at the time of the best tides. Now you might see schools of 8 to 15 tarpon coming down the same bank.

Today, I don't believe our tarpon population has decreased that much. But the fishing has changed, because 40 years ago, those big schools would come into the shallow water year after year and get into areas that had lots of food and solitude.

With the coming of fast, far-ranging skiffs sporting large outboard motors, those rich, undisturbed areas have become few and far between for the tarpon. I believe they spend more time in the deeper offshore waters. I also believe that many of those larger schools of tarpon that venture inshore are run over many times by boats with large engines, breaking them up into the smaller, more aware schools. I really don't believe tarpon have to go into shallow water to survive, but historically they did so for the easy living that the shallows provided.

Now the fish are more scattered, the schools and pods of fish smaller. And many of the biggest and the best are staying offshore.

My "good old days" of tarpon fishing have come and gone, long ago. You might not realize it, but yours are here now. Different, yes. But they're all yours, and I hope you don't waste them with negative thinking.

If you never believe another word I tell you, trust me on this: Your good old days are right now!

You have my best wishes for more and bigger fishes!

—*Stu Apte*

PHILANTHROPY

We at Stonefly Press feel that it's important to view ourselves as a small part of a greater system of balance. We give back to that which nourishes us because it feels natural and right.

Stonefly Press will be donating a portion of our annual profits to conservation groups active in environmental stewardship. We encourage all our readers to learn more about them here, and encourage you to go a step further and get involved.

American Rivers
(americanrivers.org)

California Trout
(caltrout.org)

Bonefish & Tarpon Trust
(bonefishtarpontrust.org)

Coastal Conservation Association
(joincca.org)

Riverkeeper
(riverkeeper.org)

Friends of the White River
(friendsofwhiteriver.org)

Trout Unlimited
(tu.org)

Western Rivers Conservancy
(westernrivers.org)

Index

Pflueger Taxidermy, 216
taxidermists, 216
Terry, Lord Tony, 98–99
trailing incoming tide, 78
travel issues, 113
traveling, carry-on restrictions, 112
traveling with emergency tackle
billfish tube flies, 112
camera and personal items, 113
passport photos, 112
size 5/0 or 6/0 hooks, 112
"wet bag," 113
trolling baits, 171
Tropic Star Lodge, 49. *See also* Club de Pesca
Panama
trout. *See also* brown trout; New Zealand brown
trout
flies for, 134
saltwater trout, 118
Stu Apte on, 11–12
Truman, Bess, 77–79
Truman, Harry S., 77–80
tube lure, 83
Twain, Mark, 165
Twilight Beauty patterns, 61

U
Ulysses (vessel), 139
Uslan, Nat, 95, 96

V
Valdene, Guy, 17–18, 23–27

W
wahoo, 151, 153, 155
wallabies, 101
watching choice, 210
water clarity, 69
weather, 12
"wee lures," 60
weedless spoon-worm lure, 55
Wejebe, José, 35, 37, 39, 219
wet flies versus dry flies, 98–99
Whelan, Paul, 139
Whitaker, Bob, 38, 41, 43–44

Wide World of Sports (television series), 108
wild pigs, 101, 105
Williams, Ted
"Bush," nickname for Stu Apte, 90–91
lifelong friendship with Stu Apte, 90–92
shows Stu Apte fishing spot, 30
snook fishing, 86
Stu Apte meets, 86–92
tackle choices, 86
Thanksgiving dinners, 116, 121
world record. *See also specific fish*
with 12-pound-class tippet, 47, 83
for barracuda, 83
fly rod tarpon, 26
saltwater fly rod, 47
scale for, 43
worms
chartreuse plastic, 54–55, 57
Texas rigged plastic worm, 186
weedless spoon-worm, 55
Wulff, Joan, 35
Wulff, Lee, 48, 157, 213

Y
Yastrzemski, Carl, "Yaz," 123–124
bow and arrow cast, 122
champion performance, 121–122
skish lure batting, 122
with Stu Apte, 120
Ted Williams 400 Spinning Rod, 122
Yeager, Scottie
ballyhoo teaser, 171
footage of, 48
IWFA record, 173
Pacific sailfish, 168–171
plug-casting tackle, 171
polarized glasses, 171
sailfish gaffed, 172–173
sailfish hooked, 172
yellowfin tuna, 172
yellowfin tuna, 22, 48, 142, 172

Z
Zuckerman, Steve, 140–141

Jeannine Apte with a potential female angler's world-record Pacific sailfish on a fly rod in Costa Rica.